Praise for October Child:

"*October Child* is stunningly frank and urgently told. Linda Boström Knausgård writes with what appears to be a willingness to expose herself utterly. This makes for a painful and powerful book that asks complicated questions of its readers and acknowledges the impossibility of simple answers. An extraordinary work."
CHRIS POWER, author of *Mothers: Stories*

"*October Child* is a bold book, not in its openness but in its aloofness, in its faithfulness to literature and language rather than to reason and science. Against the great story of psychiatry with its simple, ready-made answer, Boström Knausgård insists on the irrationality of humans and on the suffering of each individual."
Göteborgs-Posten

"Linda Boström Knausgård's *October Child* drove the breath from my lungs. I can't recall when I last read a novel that struck me and held me fast in this manner."
Expressen

"*October Child* is a desperate reckoning with psychiatric care. But it is also an ingeniously composed novel with mercilessly beautiful language."
Sydsvenskan

"As expected, language that is self-assured and lyrical, but in an unexpectedly acute and polemical novel."
Kulturnytt i P1

"Linda Boström Knausgård's prose moves seamlessly and evocatively between worlds. She writes as if in a dream. It's eerie and gripping."
Aftonbladet

"Linda Boström Knausgård writes with her usual linguistic momentum, a kind of inviting energy in her voice. She balances her desperation with poetic precision and makes the urgency real for the reader."
Svenska Dagbladet

"Linda Boström Knausgård creates images and scenes with a vibrant presence and her language often takes lovely poetic turns."
Dagens Nyheter

"Intense and painful."
Jönköpings-Posten

"Linda Boström Knausgård's language is like water: occasionally it pours, sometimes it solidifies to ice. As a reader, I am frozen in her despair."
Borås Tidning

"In this turmoil of darkest emotions, one marvels at the clarity of the prose. Throughout her internment, the author asks herself a question: Will I be able to write again? Do I have what it takes? The simple and quick answer to that question is, *Yes*."
Östersund Post

"A bloodcurdling memorial work, as if secretly written from a bedside. It is a difficult read, painful because it is at once so insightful and despairing, so hopeless and written in a frightening anger that spares no one, least of all the narrator. It is less literary than Boström Knausgård's previous work, and perhaps precisely because of this, in its vulnerable non-perfection, it is so overwhelming. One cannot forget it."
SVT Nyheter

•

Praise for Welcome to America:

"Here, restraint and ambiguity prevail, whether it's about the intensity of the abuse Ellen sustained or the veracity of her assertions. Regardless, it's a taut portrait of how difficult it can be to reconcile ideals about faith and family with their messier realities. An intense, recursive book that evokes the chill despair of a Bergman film."
Kirkus Reviews

"Knausgård is an impressive writer, who has created a unique, powerful lead in a world all her own."
Publishers Weekly

"A piercing story of a girl who responds to trauma by mustering the most powerful weapon available to her: silence. Melodic, mythological, transformative, a testament to literature's powers."
Vanity Fair

"Every word is there for a reason."
MinnPost

"A singular and thought-provoking story with a child narrator you won't soon forget."
Book Riot

"Knausgård's story of a family in crisis is shocking and imaginative. Everything is written in beautiful and sparse prose which suggests that, after all, from darkness comes light."
JURY, AUGUST PRIZE

"Knausgård's artistry is masterful."
Bookslut

"*Welcome to America* presents itself as an étude in the musical sense of the term: a basic theme that

varies to infinity, acquiring with each new variation a new unprecedented facet. A triumph."
Le Monde

"The incandescent *Welcome to America* allows one to discover the author's vibrant and powerful universe."
Lire

"Gets you in the gut. A delirious dance."
L'Alsace Quotidien

"A tender novel about a mute girl: gentle, sensitive, minimal, concise, subtle, and brutal. This is writing as self-defense and liberation."
VOLKER WEIDERMANN, *Spiegel*

"A daring and disturbing novel. One will not soon forget the eleven-year-old narrator and her silence."
MDR Kultur

"In her slim book, Boström Knausgård conjures a constellation reminiscent of a psychological thriller. *Welcome to America* is a book that masterfully describes the many nuances of inner darkness."
Austria Presse Agentur (APA)

"A short, very lyrical novel. The scenes succeed in their great universality, closely observed, wisely questioned."
Brigitte Woman

"Outstanding psychological chamber play. Linda Boström Knausgård has an incredible ability to give voice to the young narrator's haunting thoughts and she does it through such dense prose that is both simple and powerful, both tangible and poetic."

Politiken

"Boström Knausgård has her own poetic language. The imagery is just as natural and brilliant as it is mad and askew."

Dagbladet

"A great book! Linda Boström Knausgård certainly does not shy away from the dark and horrible in her family dramas. Her prose is beautiful, clear, and precise. I really love this novel."

Aftonbladet

"A book cannot, like a person, be accomplished. But Linda Boström Knausgård manages to get very close. She keeps her balance perfectly: She never judges, never justifies. She just narrates, with perfection."

Sydsvenskan

"Linda Boström Knausgård erases herself from her own writing. What remains is the girl who communicates directly with the reader in a remarkably strong voice, despite her being so quiet."

Svenska Dagbladet

"Hers is a way of writing that takes risks, without considering the consequences, heading straight for the unknown. Reading her novella is like experiencing a condensed depiction of decay, a decay that also carries a light so strong that it is like standing in the middle of a ray of sunshine."
Jönköpings-Posten

•

Praise for The Helios Disaster:

"*The Helios Disaster* continues the tradition of Charlotte Perkins Gilman ("The Yellow Wallpaper"), Kate Chopin (*The Awakening*), Sylvia Plath (*The Bell Jar*), and William Styron (*Darkness Visible*) in its palpable longing to communicate something about mental illness. The approach here weds sensuous imagery to taut sentences, establishing an economy of language that perhaps surpasses Boström Knausgård's predecessors in giving shape to emotion and suffering from the inside. This poignant book is important; its author, courageous."
Rain Taxi Review of Books

"In brilliant, harrowing pages of deep interiority, Knausgård describes Anna's fever dream of alienation; Anna is desperate for love and confounded by it, and chronically incapable of connecting with those who might provide it. Knausgård's bluntly surreal style—she is also a poet—suits Anna's vibrant, tormented imagination. Tidy endings are nowhere to be found; Knausgård instead gratifies by portraiture, in her thrilling conception of a young goddess on earth."

Publishers Weekly

"A moving trip to an emotional bottom. A flinty, lyrical, and storm-clouded study of loss."

Kirkus Reviews

"Linda Boström Knausgård's *The Helios Disaster* vibrates with a strange, seductive intensity. A mythological origin story as well as a modern story of otherness, it portrays the push and pull of human connection—the anguish of yearning for, but also fearing, the warmth and reach of others. Knausgård's simple, disarming words bear complex, profound, and surprising truths."

CHIA-CHIA LIN, author of *The Unpassing*

"Blending psychological realism with a hallucinatory dose of the mythological, Linda Boström Knausgård's *The Helios Disaster* eludes easy classification. It's a slim novel that moves from trauma to revelation and back again; it's also a disconcerting

reworking of some memorable myths and legends. Running throughout the novel is a measured consideration of belief and humanity's relationship to the divine—both metaphorically and literally."
Words Without Borders

"Boström Knausgård is good at evoking the fragility that can afflict even the most loving families. Her sentences, translated from the Swedish by Rachel Willson-Broyles, are short, dry and brittle, like tinder on the verge of combustion. The writing then takes fire in the desperate and disturbing portrait of mental illness."
Wall Street Journal

"Knausgård's interpretation of a young Athena will indeed resonate for those readers familiar with narratives of teenage depression and suicide, as well as join those other worthy literary revisions of legendary gods whose exposed humanity in our world makes them more human than the mortals they are forced to commiserate with."
The Literary Review

"The emotional intensity created by Boström Knausgård recalls Sylvia Plath, but her spare, accelerating modern myth owes something to the poet/classicist Anne Carson's novels in verse. This novella cannot be read quickly, its psycho-

logical range and febrile prose demand attentiveness. It takes skill and imagination to describe extreme emotions in ways to which everybody can relate but that's what Boström Knausgård achieves in this short, piercing book."
The Independent

"This intriguing, lyrical novel is a powerful portrait of mental illness."
Times Literary Supplement

"The story is tightly, cleverly organized around a central idea: to show how Anna's perceptive, disturbed mind struggles to impose some kind of mental order and, finally, fails. The author's passionate involvement with her protagonist illuminates what it is like to slide irresistibly away from reality."
Swedish Book Review

"Linda Boström Knausgård's style is magical, hallucinatory, and very poetic. Passionate, refined, and as clear as cool water."
Aftonbladet

"The strangeness, originality, and supreme gentleness of the narrator's inner world contrast sharply with the more recognizable, though not in all respects ordinary world into which she is forced.

This, combined with her quiet determination to find her father and the increasingly astonishing events that occur, all add up to form a surprisingly modern portrait of longing and the possibility of homecoming."
Bookslut

"*The Helios Disaster* is a story about longing for a father and about prepubescence. About the will to die, refusal, and a sun shining far too brightly. But in this field of tension there is also a simple happiness. Boström Knausgård's authorship keeps getting better and better."
Dagens Nyheter

"It is simple and it is grand, a story about a girl who came too close to the sun. *The Helios Disaster* shines!"
Kulturnytt i P1

"*The Helios Disaster* is an insightful story about mental illness and missing a father. Linda Boström Knausgård manages to fill the rather monotonous hospital existence with a tension so powerful and poetic that one is actually quite taken by it and reads it without missing a single detail."
Kulturnyheterna SVT

"*The Helios Disaster* is a dense, tender, painful novel written in a prose which, always poetic, touches, shakes, and makes a mess."

Helsingborgs Dagblad

"Chosen for the unsentimental language of her portrayal of human existence on the border between a world distorted by psychosis and reality's structured existence. Her stories are written according to the logic of myths, never asking why, but allowing an understanding of ourselves that is difficult to be determined in the dominant categories."

JURY, MARE KANDRE PRIZE

OCTOBER CHILD

LINDA BOSTRÖM KNAUSGÅRD

OCTOBER CHILD

Translated from the Swedish
by Saskia Vogel

WORLD EDITIONS
New York, London, Amsterdam

Published in the USA in 2021 by World Editions LLC, New York
Published in the UK in 2021 by World Editions Ltd., London

World Editions
New York | London | Amsterdam

Printed by Lake Book, USA

Library of Congress Cataloging in Publication Data is available

ISBN 978-1-64286-089-4

First published as *Oktoberbarn* in Sweden in 2019 by Modernista. Published by agreement with Copenhagen Literary Agency ApS, Copenhagen.

The cost of this translation was defrayed by a subsidy from the Swedish Arts Council, gratefully acknowledged.

Twitter: @WorldEdBooks
Facebook: @WorldEditionsInternationalPublishing
Instagram: @WorldEdBooks
www.worldeditions.org

Book Club Discussion Guides are available on our website.

I wish I could tell you all about the factory, but I can't anymore. And soon I'll no longer be able to remember my days or nights or why I was born. This is what I know: I was there for several long stretches between 2013 and 2017 and my brain was shot through with so much electricity that they were sure I wouldn't be able to write this. *We'll start with an intensive series of twelve treatments.* This was their word for it. Treatments. A word to neutralize their venture and reduce the fear around the procedure. They said it was a gentle treatment, like restarting a computer. Yes, they really did use such awful imagery. Theirs was a language created by people who believe that this method can in fact relieve a person's suffering, and they were so used to it that the procedure became something as easily forgotten as your most recent lie. They carried out twenty procedures a day. These conveyor-belt affairs were the crowning glory of a business devoid of insight. In here they had free rein, and could explain away a person dropping out by saying that he or she wasn't responding to the treatment. Under such circumstances, results were proudly discussed instead. Every gap of contact with the outside world was sealed off. They were so afraid of scrutiny that they blamed everything on the patient. She was unmanageable. He was already too far gone. She was desperate. The old woman was chronic and should have been living in another time, when she could have resided peacefully with the others in a world adapted to each of their individual needs. Three hours' conditional discharge in the park and an always-sympathetic nurse's hands. That time had passed. Nowadays no one wanted chronics on their ward. Results were what mattered, and what got results was the ever-so-popular electroconvulsive therapy—the answer to a person's every torment. They sold their treatments to patients who had no choice but to believe what the chief physician was saying in the brief time there actually was to discuss it. Ten minutes a week, no time for questions. Difficult patients were given a higher voltage. Everybody knew that.

I had a weakness inside me and all throughout my being, so I ended up at this place a lot. I'd been subjected to electricity a number of times. I knew everything about the treatment.

At five o'clock in the morning a nurse would come into the room to insert a needle. By the way the door handle was grabbed you could tell whether or not it was going to hurt. Zahid was afraid of inserting needles, so he'd always miss and would start sweating right there in the little room. Maybe it was no surprise he'd miss, as weak as the lamplight was in that room. How the others found the blood in my veins seemed like a wonder in this half-light. Finally Zahid would slide the needle into the back of my hand, where the veins were most prominent but where it hurt the patient most. If Sister Maria opened the door you knew you wouldn't feel a thing. The needle slid in painlessly, and she received many grateful smiles. Aalif would jam the needle in. He had perfect aim and for this we were grateful, but his jamming hurt so much that for a while the pain would wipe out whatever reality you happened to be in. Some poked around without hitting their mark, the veins forever rolling away. Remarkably, veins always rolled for the same people. And some would stick it in without warning. Those times I'd scream in pain. I needed to prepare myself for the needle's entry. I needed to hear *Here it comes* so I could exhale when the needle pushed through the skin and so magically ward off the pain. Or at least render it manageable. When the needle was in place they taped on an injection port, which they then flushed through with saline to make sure the cannula worked and the anesthesia had free access, both to your bodily functions and to your mind, which would give up at once. Total capitulation.

Let's back up. To what landed you there. You were never allowed to walk there alone. An orderly was always by your side, and usually Aalif was the one who fetched me. I liked Aalif. Nothing wrong with him. He came from a hotter country and had fled war. We would walk together for maybe twenty meters. First out of the ward, then three steps to the left and into the short tunnel that led to the factory.

We sat in a waiting room all in a row, we who were to be treated and our chaperones. The pace in there was breakneck. They were organized. They managed, as I've mentioned, to squeeze in twenty poor souls each morning. We sat in the waiting room and I said nothing for the most part, but if my blood was pumping faster than usual we'd talk about Aalif's homeland. I'd ask him about the war and if it wasn't awful being in this country, where no one sat outside at night and where conversations were only ever about whether you were someone who could be counted on, or whether you weren't someone who could be counted on. Aalif responded with a gesture that meant *what can you do* and said: It's better here. Better for the family.

Often I just sat there and stared at the door, which opened at regular intervals, and a pressed and polished blond medical student with white teeth would call out a name and either you'd stay put on the waiting room bench, or, if it was your name being called, you would get up and walk into the room with your chaperone.

Once inside, there was no time for doubt. Up on the gurney. The anesthesiologist: Have you had anything to eat or drink today? Do you have any loose teeth?

Blood pressure was measured while the nurse affixed electrodes to the top of your chest and forehead. Then a student arrived with the oxygen that you had to inhale in order to saturate the brain. The anesthesiologist would say soon you'll be sleeping and then the cold anesthesia was injected into the blood through the pre-prepared cannula. Like drinking darkness.

Aalif told me what came next, once you were asleep. First they inserted a bite guard to keep you from biting your tongue. Muscle relaxant was injected through the cannula to prevent the body from flailing around on the cot. This is why the voltage had to be high, to provoke a seizure. The part with the electricity was quick. The electricity in which they trusted. The electricity that was the doctors' salvation. The side-effect-free electricity that would provide relief no medicine could.

The electricity that for anything from a few seconds to a minute would cause the convulsions that were the very key to a successful treatment.

What happened once the seizure was through is a story for another time, but I'll say this much: all us patients lay side by side on narrow cots, so close we were almost touching. Each and every one of us in our own darkness in a sleep that can't be understood. And so we slept, behind a curtain. It was important not to let the patient entering the room see the sleepers. It was important not to scare anyone before this gentle treatment. Nonetheless, I'd glimpsed the sleepers many times, and the thought that soon I'd be the one lying there, one among many, unaware of what was going on around me, frightened me more than the electricity itself.

Nobody cared that I wouldn't be able to remember large swathes of time afterwards. Memory loss was offset by the effect of the treatment. And what is the weight of memory? How can it be measured? How do you assign value to memories? Memories had a low status in the factory. They'd rather give you four weeks of voltage than have you wobbling around the ward for months on end.

It was intoxicating for those who worked with the outer edges of a person to finally be able to produce results, and so be invited into finer company.

I was an author by this point. Miserable work. No relief. No comfort. No rest. No joy. Only strong memories of where I'd written, fantasies and words sometimes hitting the mark. I wrote so infrequently it was ridiculous to call myself an author, but I did anyway. "Author" was my Plan B. Plan A was to be an actress, at which I tried my hand in my early youth. My talent was patchy. Some nights I excelled, completely free on stage, and then the joy I'd feel was indescribable. There were no words for that relief. Being free and still knowing exactly what was going to happen. Protected among others, but still my own person. Paradise on earth.

Still, it didn't feel like my choice, my own personal conquest. My mother had discovered the profession, and ultimately I didn't want to follow in her footsteps. The theater was also made unbearable by those nights when I'd stumble over my lines, like a talentless amateur, anxiety my only companion. I knew such patchiness wouldn't cut it in this profession. Reason told me to give up on my dream and choose what had always been there. Writing.

I wrote more in my childhood than I do now. I have nothing to say. I'm also having some sort of crisis. Not just the treatments and the days spent walking up and down the hallways, but me being completely without protection.

I am alone with myself. I have no friends in the city I live in and my husband has left me. He tired of being the person who held all the conversations with the children around the table. He piled on the jokes to hide the fact that I never spoke. Not during meals and not otherwise either. With the exception of when I'd rattle on endlessly. I was gone a lot.

Was often at this hospital. My illness dragged us all down. He hadn't wanted this existence. Love became an itchy sweatshirt that had to go. Get rid of that sweater and everything would be fine again.

I didn't pray in those years. Had I forgotten to pray for a lifelong love? Can I blame my neglect on anything? Why didn't I behave better during our life together?

I don't know.

You know how many different moods I can harbor at any given time. It got worse towards the end.

I choose to see this newness as a test from God.

In high school I had done two big projects, one about Sophocles and the other about Job from the Bible. I imagine that I have entered the age of Job.

Duty, toil, and heaven's closed door.

One day I found myself alone in a house, unsure of how to continue my life. I was worthless because nobody loved me, and I couldn't manage anything alone. The loneliness was potent and I couldn't figure out how to live my life, so I ended up living the life of no one. I was nobody. Pretending to live, of course, although I wasn't really. I fantasized about disappearing, or dying by my own hand, but making it look like an accident. I searched the web for how best to stage an accident. I must've also inquired online about how to get a hold of a weapon, because the US Army started messaging me; the first thing they wrote was: *You can't stand all this freedom*. And they were right about that. This freedom was not for me. Next they wrote that for a tidy sum anything could be bought in their shop. This is when I realized it wasn't the US Army writing to me, but a weaponry store of the same name. If I imagine taking my own life, shooting myself seems the easiest way to go. This I could do, but it would be hard to make it seem like someone else had shot me, so with a certain measure of sadness I started exploring other options. I was too cowardly for them all. I couldn't jump from a great height and I couldn't swallow all those pills I had, an option stashed away in a metal box. One time I made contact with the underworld. I rode the train into the big city at the edge of the miserable world in which I lived. I knew where to go. Everyone did. I walked up to the person with the biggest entourage and asked what it would cost to have someone push me in front of a train. I had been awarded a stipend and this was the amount I had at my disposal. He laughed at the amount. Who would risk their freedom for that nothing sum? he asked me, and if I ever bothered him again I'd better have a hundred times that amount. I left with my tail between my legs. Who was I? Where had I ended up and how could I get out?

I focused on the children. I cooked food from scratch and held them as close as I could. Still, they were biding their time with me. The older ones longed to be back with their dad. We had better contact over the phone when they were with him and this was a comfort, even if the admonishments were always there. It was my fault. I was the one who'd split us all up.

The younger ones wanted to be with me and I was allowed to be close to them, and fulfilling their every wish felt a lot like joy. I was good with the young ones and worse with the older ones, who demanded real answers to their questions. Not my pretend ones. I wasn't fully present, sunk as I was in a no-man's-land from where I couldn't see the possibility of a real life. One big problem was that I didn't dare grieve. I refused to appear as the loser I was. No tears. It was okay, I told myself. I didn't want his way of measuring distance anyway. And I meant it. But I was even more serious about my own paralysis.

While this was happening a book I'd written was doing well. It was confusing. A type of joy in the midst of the hurt, which I pretended didn't exist. Publishing books is not for troubled souls. At least not for a troubled soul in need.

After a few months there was an emergency hospitalization.

I had taken the night train up to meet with my editor Kristofer. Together we were going to cancel half of everything I'd agree to do. I'd made a mess of things. That very night I was supposed to be both in Oslo and in Washington. And there were a few other author events and visits to libraries planned. Nothing that couldn't be postponed.

On the other hand, there were certain things I wouldn't dream of canceling. I was supposed to go to Jerusalem with two other authors and the woman who'd organized the trip. We were going to have a reading at a café then go on to Tel Aviv and visit Amos Oz in his home. I'd started reading up on Amos Oz: *In the Land of Israel, A Tale of Love and Darkness.*

The nice part was that we were promised a lot of free time to explore the cities. I'd read about Jerusalem all my adult life. I didn't want to miss a thing. I was going to walk around the holy city between the holy places. For some reason I was sure I had a viable idea for a play. I'd received a commission from a theater, but couldn't find a way to begin. I was dreaming up a play that addressed the common point of origin of the three world religions. I wanted to elaborate on one story in particular, I won't say which. It would be strange to see old Jerusalem in proximity to the usual brands popping up across the globe at lightning speed. There would be a clash, and I'd have to make sure not to let it affect me. I had taken up the Bible again.

Bought yet another tourist guide for Jerusalem.

Really, I didn't know as much about Jerusalem as I pretended to. There were historical gaps, but I'd probably have enough time to prepare.

Early one morning I was going to wake up and press my forehead to the Wailing Wall and ask for help.

I arrived at Central Station early in the morning and the next thing I remember is standing in an antiquarian bookshop admiring three icons surrounded by books on a table in front of me. I bought all three of them with money I didn't have. I am full of joy. The Archangel Gabriel. Michael. St. George and the Dragon. I have found the protection I've been longing for and I leave the antiquarian bookshop full of reassurance. So, this is what you call a turning point. From now on my life is changed. This is what the icons are telling me. The next thing I remember is removing Kristofer's pin. The pin he always wears, the one with 1984 written on it, and on this special occasion I take it to be my year.

It's my pin now. I take it and I'm sitting in a waiting room with gold hanging from the ceiling. When I wake up my mother comes over to me. I lie down on a bed and she comes to me as she has come to me eight, eleven, or thirty times before, and she pets my hair and I am at the hospital and she is visiting me and everything is as always. It's just that I'm in the wrong city.

What is your usual care facility? It's important for you to be where they know you. As if anyone in their industry could ever get to know you. The people who know me are my ex-husband, and who else? Not the people in the waterside ward, in any case. They make a phone call and I am driven to the air ambulance and three people spend the entire flight looking at me. They're looking at me the whole time, while I'm strapped to a gurney and wondering what they think I'm going to do: Hijack the plane? Fly it into a mountain? That's exactly what I would do if I wasn't so cowardly and lacking in imagination.

I was given VIP treatment upon entering the factory. A quick and decisive adjustment was needed.

I slept my fill and when I woke up I didn't know who I was, where I was, or why. They took three of my nine lives that time. And I'd already done away with five, so that left me with one. They just took them like it was nothing.

Eighteen treatments. I don't remember much. Barely anything. They don't care about that. It surprises me that I care, but I do. I'll take it up with whichever chief physician is present for those ten minutes I'm owed. It's never the same chief physician; nobody wants to stay in this ward that reeks of confusion and fear. Only certain care workers and nurses were constant: Zahid, Aalif, Sister Maria, Christian who I play chess with, Lennart, and Muhammed who sometimes appears like a god among us mortals. He circled the wards, was called in where there was the most violence. Like the time Thobias was going to hit me because I happened to pass by his open door at the very moment he was thinking of his wife.

It was summer and sunny this time and the ward was sweating in the heat let in by the plastic windows, and the young one, I'll call him Trudy, and I had claimed the barred-in balcony at the end of the corridor as our refuge. I went on about how pretty the ferries were, gliding back and forth across the sound, and about our vexing proximity to Kronborg Castle, where Hamlet had lived.

Can you imagine being so close to the castle and still never having been there? It's audacious, an offense, indolence, practically a mortal sin.

What are you talking about? the young one said, and looked out over the water. I realized then and there that he was the first person I'd ever met who didn't know who Hamlet was. Standing in the sun behind the bars placed there to prevent you from throwing yourself off the balcony, I considered telling him about Hamlet, but what would I say?

Hamlet was a young prince who lost his father, and at midnight his father's ghost told him that the father had been murdered by his uncle, who'd swiftly married the queen, Hamlet's own mother. Take that.

Trudy—he hated being called that—put his face close to mine. I backed up and stuffed him full of Hamlet quotations, because in all honesty he made me nervous. A youth with everything a youth has on his heart.

Time is out of joint; O, cursed spite, That ever I was born to set it right. To be or not to be. Sicklied o'er with the pale cast of thought.

Trudy turned my face towards his. I decided to forget about Hamlet. I experienced a levity, an intoxication there in the light pared by the bars and I turned my back to Öresund, and the young man's face was so close to mine, and we kissed.

Our long kiss might have softened me up because when Thobias caught sight of me as I passed by his open door and he immediately came to think of his wife and then shouted *whore* at me, I spun around and walked over to him. Thobias stood up, and had the young man not been behind me he'd have beat me until I lay in a heap on the floor, and then he would've kept on kicking. The young man was a kickboxer and dared step up to the now-silent Thobias and it all ended with Thobias sitting back down on the bed, the incident over before it had begun. I remember thinking that it was the first time anyone had come to my defense. In my youth when I'd been in situations that ended in violence, the men I'd spent my time with had held *me* back when I'd been attacked, instead of us taking revenge together and beating down the person who'd humiliated me in front of everyone. His name had been Thobias too, the short, aggressive actor who, at a party, had also called me a whore. This, after I'd asked him to not be so rude to me and my friends. I put my cigarette out on his cheek in reply and he hit me. A clean right hook.

Maybe I should finally accept that Thobiases aren't the best company to keep. But what about my former colleague Thobias? He was very sympathetic. Does character alone determine how you carry your name?

Thobias-in-the-ward fixated on me and wanted to hit me on sight, and so Muhammed was called in. Thobias was 190 cm tall, mute, and locked in a rage that meant even Muhammed had to give it his all. They couldn't keep him strapped down all the time. There were rules for everything. Muhammed, who was also a kickboxer and had competed at a high level, established a sense of calm in the ward that at least I thought I appreciated. Two meters tall and with that walk of his, he didn't seem human, and the first time I saw him I said:

You don't look like you're of this world.

Muhammed was calm personified and I stayed close to him when Thobias neared. Yes, I stayed close to him most of the time.

Often he sat around reading a book in Arabic and when he heard a fight break out, he'd finish the paragraph before setting the book aside and getting up to, with his mere presence, restore the peace. Lagging, but attuned to whatever he would encounter.

I talked and talked with Muhammed about anything and everything. Days like nights and nights like days, the lack of seasons in here, the food, the boiled vegetables that tasted of water, the boredom and understanding, the loneliness. I asked him if he'd ever been in the factory and he took a long look at me before asking:

What do you mean?

Have you never gone through that door

and taken those three steps to the left that lead into the tunnel?

Muhammed thought about it, which I appreciated.

Do you mean here at the hospital?

Yes, have you been in the room where first they knock you out and then they try to wake you up like a newborn with the electricity? Have you ever rolled the sleepers through that ward?

Yes, I have, he replied. I work here.

Muhammed left and I thought, like so many times before, that no one wants to be in my company. Not even the worms that haunt me at night. They're everywhere. How long have I been dead? Am I buried and how long have I lain underground? Did I scare Muhammed away? I felt ashamed. I'd pressured him. Why would someone like him want to talk to someone like me? Surely he had other things to do. What do I care about Muhammed? Screw him. Why was he working here if he was such a high-ranking kickboxer? Muhammed is nothing to me. A nobody with no clue about how to help others in moments of difficulty. This, even though he was a care worker and that was his job.

I was in the middle of this thought when he returned and sat back down. Maybe he'd just gone to the toilet.

My joy over his return obliterated the shame in an instant. I hadn't been rejected. He'd endured my nonsense and everything was as before. Something like a shiver of joy ran through my body. I'd spent years practicing not giving in to my impulses. I'd learned to be still when a thought came charging. I was more composed now. Not so over the top all the time. I was here on a visit. Wasn't I?

All the things I'd said and hadn't done washed over me as I sat, tormented, in my darkness. I was soiled with hyperbole and lies. My lies. Sitting here was out of the question. I had to get up and get out. Go to my room if nothing else. I could probably come up with something to do. I was suddenly full of ideas. Cross-breezes and invulnerability. Can I say that? Doesn't sound good. Forget it. This haunt suddenly felt like a landscape in miniature. I was a giant come walking, everyone else was a Lilliputian. They only had seconds to live. All I had to do was put my foot down.

No, I was the one who was tiny beneath the sky I hadn't seen in so long. Only through the bars on the balcony where I'd still ask for a cigarette sometimes if I had company; if I was by myself I'd search through the large plant pot full of earth. There were lots of barely smoked cigarettes to be found—smoking was forbidden out there, after all. Yes, yes. What does this have to do with anything? Stop searching the ground for crumbs. It's enough. It's enough now.

Just to have said something, I said:

Muhammed is the god who smiles but cannot love.

Where did you get that from?

I answered truthfully: A Palestinian poet said that to me once, though only after I'd asked him. I'd really pressed that man for knowledge, right before he was supposed to go on stage and read his poems no less.

A Palestinian poet. I understand.

Is Muhammed the god who smiles but cannot love?

The prophet, Muhammed said, and kept

reading. Muhammed is the prophet.

Yes, that's what I said, I said.

Why don't I have it in me to think just a little before I speak? Why do I speak at all?

Can't you love? I continued.

Does it look like I'm smiling?

You might be smiling on the inside.

Not right now I'm not, Muhammed said, and got up and went to the office, which was nearby. Only a few steps away.

I'm not bothered about Muhammed. I have more important things to do than sit here and expose myself. I don't intend to say anything. Nothing is what I intend to say. I closed my eyes, forced my thoughts to stop like I'd learned to do as a child, and fell asleep immediately. I slept an innocent sleep where nothing scared me. Everything was as usual. My husband was sleeping next to me. It was night. I got up and visited the children, who were sleeping. They were always such deep sleepers. I took their hands in mine. I spent a long time looking at them. The girls' fanned-out, tangled hair, their cheeks. The boy's pale face. They were so beautiful. Still unaware of what would happen when they woke up.

How all of us would sit around the table and you'd say that we were getting divorced. We've grown apart, you'd say. It's going to be fine, was all I could muster, not actually knowing anything. Nothing about what would happen once we got up. Or in six months, or a year. What would we do then? Someone tell me. It is of the utmost importance that I find out as much as possible. Three weeks have passed since you announced it. I mean, a year and a half.

I walked down the stairs where the cat was sleeping. Our Siberian Forest cat. She who never wanted to lay in anyone's lap and dug her claws in if you tried to carry her. She brought home prey, each more impressive than the last. Once an animal we couldn't identify lay outside our door, its throat slit. A ferret? No, not a ferret? Aren't they small? A roadkill badger? Impossible to see because the body was so battered. You fetched the camera and shot the prey. The sight enlivened you. I don't know why you had to take a picture all of a sudden. You never did otherwise. I was the one who took pictures. Developed and enlarged photos of the children and put them in albums. When did I stop? We only had printed photos of the children up to a certain age. I suddenly felt worried. I have to start taking pictures again. There has to be continuity. They have to be able to see themselves. How they grew. Anna, who'd always sit in the tree with her best friend, talking, exactly as I had done in the park I would escape to. Escape? Why are you always so dramatic? Didn't you go there to buy ice cream in the spring like everybody else?

I have to wake him!

I have to get him to understand that he's the only one who wants this. Not the children and not me. You have to explain, I said. You can't present a fact like that and then shut up. Why not? you said. I do as I please.

I went back into the bedroom and lay down next to your body. You slept like a stone. You didn't notice that I had lain down next to you. I took your arm and laid it over me. I thought of our first winter when we sledded down the sand dunes on the beach.

Our early astonishment over the unknown landscape. It was like nothing we'd ever experienced. The sun on the snow and the water. The horizon, the Polish ferry a distant speck. When you tested to see if sledding was possible, you zipped down the dunes, out onto the beach, and right into the sea.

Muhammed nudges my shoulder. I open my eyes, wide awake. Muhammed's eyes. How to describe their color? Sometimes brown like blood. Or like thought. Black gold. I wonder how it feels to be like him? Sure I can handle whatever life brings me.

Up onto the floor, he said. I stayed put.

Now. His voice was far away. I barely heard what he was saying.

Me?

Yes. You.

I get up. Muhammed hands me a jump rope. Where did he get it? Like everyone else, he knows jump ropes aren't allowed here. A jump rope is an excellent tool for someone who's thinking about Last Exit Sweden all day long, the very last exit in Sweden before you helplessly drive up on the bridge to Denmark, the land of freedom. Yes, any final step at all. Hamlet was following me and had now manifested in this jump rope. No. I refuse.

Do they think I'm this easily tricked?

Here, it paid to not be paranoid and see signs everywhere, but to be very clear-minded.

I take the jump rope and a number of possibilities appear. Is Muhammed giving me a way out?

No, no, and again no.

Can I trick him?

Jump. Muhammed looks angry, of course, and he has every right to be. Surely he can read my mind. My God. Poor Muhammed.

You need to move. Jump.

No one tells me what to do. No way am I going to jump.

I jump.

I don't know why I do. We stand at the far end of the hallway closest to the exit. Maria passes by. She smiles at me and takes out her bunch of keys. This angers me. I don't smile back. I'm terrified, terrified by what I'm going to do with this jump rope. The beat of my heart. One, two, three. I can't hear anything. Muhammed counting. I can't. I can't do it. I stop. Ten, Muhammed counts. No way am I going to jump rope, I say, and hand the rope over.

Then run, Muhammed says.

Suddenly we're running through the halls. It's not allowed, I know, but running with Muhammed was special. He ran as slowly as I did. One step behind me to speed me up, to spur me on. We ran past the nurse's office with the locked medicine cabinet, onward through the corridors, past the empty day room. Why is it empty? Where is everybody? Onward past the rooms with the numbered doors. Past the closed-door meeting rooms, all the way to the doctor's office where someone was typing on a computer with their back to us. Why didn't they draw the curtain? Why this sudden exposure? We ran up to the smoking pen and turned around. Back and forth. I wanted to give up, stop after a few laps. Running in this corridor felt ridiculous. I stopped. Muhammed shoved me. I started running again. Now he was running next to me.

If you stop, you'll ruin all chance of healing, he said. In giving up, you refuse your body the chance to heal. Right when you think you've used up all your energy and want to stop, you actually have exactly as much energy left to give. Keep going. I'll say when.

It felt like we'd been running for hours. We ran up and down the corridor until it was time for the afternoon coffee break. Now the dayroom was crawling with people, people who wanted to eat store-bought baked goods and drink juice. Which I also wanted.

Once we'd finally stopped, Muhammed patted me on the shoulder. He'd wrapped the jump rope around his hand.

The days we spent running in the corridor became brighter and brighter. Clear. Free from humiliation, at least that's what I told myself. We ran past Thobias's open door; he refused to have his door closed. I'm fucking claustrophobic, he shouted into the ward. That's because you're locked in your own head, I dared shout back as we ran past him. I understand why your wife left you. You can't talk. So what if Muhammed was shushing me.

If this is how you're gonna be, I'm not going to keep running with you.

I stopped. This was your idea, I said, and

started to walk away. Muhammed caught up with me.

So shut up, he said, and started running again.

I liked teasing Thobias now that Muhammed was there. Why not? Fuck him. Muhammed, who casually shut the door when he got up to leave. A few weeks later I'd regret the words I'd flung at Thobias, but I didn't know that yet, that I'd run into him in the hospital kiosk all alone. He was friendly and said sorry and whatnot. His wife was four months pregnant. They were giving it another go, he said as he poured candy into a bag. I watched him fill the bag to the top and I who was there for the same reason dropped my candy on the floor, probably because I was scared to death.

Good, I said, and ran off.

I was shaking with fear when I reentered the ward.

Be nice to everybody, I repeated like a mantra as I sat on the bed crying. There's more than right now, there's an after too, and there you are on your own and nobody cares what happens to you.

I knew this as I was running with Muhammed, feeling invincible. Like so often when you find yourself in an unfamiliar state, you get a little relentless. Euphoric. All hurdles seem to suddenly disappear. I needed no one. No one. I was free. Master of my own happiness. I could probably turn water into fire. Temper steel. It would be fine. It would be fine in the abandoned house on the street by the old water tower, where the wind reigned free. The crows and ravens shrieked throughout the night in the park next to the house. Those wretched birds.

Why not? It's only going to get better. It's already better. What, or who, could stop me? No one could stop me. Nothing could draw me back in. The children and I would have it good. We would get even closer. Have it even better. I actually believed this wholeheartedly. I would suffer through anything because I wanted this. To transform my tedium into a victory parade. What could be won, I didn't know, but since no one was stopping my thoughts all I could do was continue. Trust. I would earn it back. Their trust, joy, and access to their dreams and fantasies. It was so easy. We would go riding on the beach and mold tin soldiers. I would never ever scare them again. In a single hour, I could swing between deep depression and euphoria. But no more! I was absolutely to be trusted. We would take the train up to my hometown and I would show them Humlegården, the National Library, the theater. We would go to children's plays, applaud, and visit the friends who still liked me.

I had only dipped my toes in here among the shadows. My contours seemed to be drawn in ink. I could stretch time. Fast forward to the day they would be forced to return me to myself and my clear fantasies. They had long since stopped the treatments. I would run out of the ward. Muhammed would help me.

*

What I didn't know was that Muhammed would soon leave the ward together with Thobias.

Thobias was being moved to another ward and the staff exhaled. Muhammed no longer needed to watch over us all day long. I mourned not being able to be near him. Why did they have to move Thobias?

As Muhammed was about to leave he said that he would pray for me, then he disappeared to the place that was calling for him. I missed him more than I should have. Muhammed had told me of things I knew nothing about. He described the Koran to me, and as he was speaking I felt that maybe this was the best place for me after all. He explained the special gifts of prayer and when I asked him if he prayed in here he said yes. How? I asked. I've never seen you pray. How do you know? he asked. His voice was the kind you wanted to listen and be close to.

But everything comes to an end.

Suddenly he was gone and when I ended up in a fight, it wasn't Muhammed who came, but another care worker with a syringe.

As I've mentioned, our ward was full of care workers.

Britt, Charlotta, Varg, Elsa, Christina, and Sofia. My favorites were Aalif and

Muhammed, of course, though I might never see Muhammed again; but Sister Maria was the one who got me to talk about what was happening inside me. Most care workers were okay, but they never questioned anything. No one wanted to get involved. No one wanted to put in a good word ahead of a doctor's visit. No one questioned why I was locked up in this ward, safekeeping, safekeeping, safekeeping, except Maria, she gave me the impression that she wanted me to be both here and at home in my own reality, following my destiny.

She was the one who'd pick me up in time to meet the chief physician face-to-face. She'd drag me out into the corridor where you had to rush after whichever doctor was at that moment making their way through the ward, all paperwork and good posture. The room he or she opened the door to was cared for by no one. A table and a few chairs, strip lights crackling on the ceiling.

I slept a silent sleep, refused to eat, died each time my head met the pillow. Did this follow a treatment from which I'd never wake, or was it a refusal? A quiet sorrow I'd never recover from? *To die* echoed in my head. To sleep, to sleep, perchance to dream.

What if death is not the end? What am I to do then?

Maria opened the door to my room one day among all the other days and said it was time. She'd notified me more than once already and if I didn't get up she'd have to call for reinforcements. I apologized and got out of bed. It had been a while. I counted my steps along the corridor to calm myself and prepare for the meeting that would barely have time to take place. By step fifty-four I was standing in front of a door that was shut as quickly as it was opened.

This ridiculous chief physician pretended to look over my file as he spoke:

After all, you must be pleased that you've come to your senses. Though there were many treatments in rapid succession, on the whole it has been a success.

I said I was an author and that I needed my memories.

Only then did he look at me and say that the memories would come back. They always do. Sooner or later. Perhaps not all of them, definitely not all of them, but it's hard, if not impossible, to find a treatment that's free of side effects. You understand, don't you? You can always make things up. Isn't that what authors do? I saw black and didn't know what to do with myself. I tried to hold back, but it ended with me flying at him and grabbing him by the throat and feeling pleased to see genuine fear in his eyes.

Of course I was punished. An escort, the sign of a patient in need of constant supervision. I started referring to them as the ss.

It was insufferable. Keeping your own cursed company is bad enough. Try doing anything when there's a care worker sitting in the same room. I couldn't read. Couldn't write. Couldn't think. It was idiotic. They took turns. It was taxing for the care worker, too, to sit there supervising.

At night the shift workers shined a flashlight on you to check if you were breathing. They came by every five minutes when you'd been assigned an escort. There was a round window on the door, so they could peer in.

The flashlights rhythmically sweeping over me throughout the night made it impossible to sleep.

First the light hit my eyes, then it roved around the room like the beam from a lighthouse in the darkness across the sea.

Sedatives and yet another series of treatments, an escort for weeks, months.

The next time I saw the doctor I'd attacked, I didn't remember him.

Sister Maria advised me to collect my memories, the sooner the better. She wasn't happy with the results of the treatment, with me being left to wander the corridors, recoiling from the slightest touch. She asked me if I remembered my children and I said, Of course I do.

What are their names? she asked.

I tried to reply, but as I was about to say *Anna* a pain spread behind my eyes, like it does before the tears push through, and once I started crying I couldn't stop.

Think of your children, said Maria, who took the tears to be a good sign. Think about what they're doing while you're here.

What are they doing right now?

As soon as she said this I started crying even harder and fell into her arms. She held me as I cried and after a while she said, Try thinking about them when they were small; those were happy times, if I've understood right?

Had my retreat been cowardly? I saw Anna, Olivia, and Josef, my husband and myself, as if in a photograph. We were on a much-longed-for vacation. My husband had been working on a book night and day until finally it was finished and what a relief it was to be normal again. Not to have to run around like a fool in the apartment in the city where we were then living. Catching the children, making them stay at the table for more than a few minutes, feeding them, putting them to bed. I thought everything was going to go back to normal. I didn't know then what I would later discover: that this was only the beginning and the end would be much worse than I could ever have imagined.

You'd booked the vacation in your sleep; you'd always wanted to go to the Maldives. It was a memorable trip with our three children and one grumpy passenger, who tried to hush the children when we didn't manage it ourselves. The children were three, five, and six years old; it's a lot to ask of them not to make a sound. I, who had a hard time curbing my aggressions, chewed out the fat, pig-eyed man whose complaints were the loudest of them all.

It's no surprise you don't know anything about small children, as I doubt any woman could ever imagine being close to you.

Not being one for public displays, you had no luck trying to calm me. It wasn't that bad, really. The children liked traveling, they were only screaming a little bit. And right then the fat man attacked, as though he'd been waiting for his chance to make his voice heard.

What do you care? Older men don't hear well anyway, do they? I said, interrupting him.

When we finally got to the hotel all we saw were palm trees and greenery, endless shadows and hills.

You looked out over the landscape and said, What the fuck is this?

It turned out we were in Mauritius and not in the Maldives, your dream destination, and I spent the entire vacation in the shade with the children, saying, Oh, how lovely it is here in Mauritius. Mauritius. Mauritius. It served him right. What would we have done in the Maldives? Especially me, who can't handle the sun.

Whatever the case, the trip was a dream and I didn't dare think of how much it had cost. Sure, my husband's books had started selling like hot cakes and so we, who'd never cared for money, who went to the pawnshop after the preschool drop-off, were rich. Well, not rich, but the pressure was off and men no longer showed up at our apartment asking questions.

This hasn't been paid, they'd say waving a bill, nor this one or this one. And this was sent to the debt collectors long ago. Do you have any assets? Art? Furniture? Undeclared property, perhaps?

What are those men called? Creditors?

My mother had taught me to be extremely genial and kind to men like these. We were living in a five-room apartment in Malmö for which we'd traded my mother's gorgeous apartment after she'd signed it over to us, two parents of small children with a tendency to flee.

You arrived in Sweden with a library in your luggage, three times the size of mine.

In this splendid apartment we mixed our books on your bookshelf for the first time.

We didn't consider that my mother would come to miss her two-room apartment on Regeringsgatan right across from the Nalen concert hall. We were the future.

You'd said you wanted a flock of children. I wanted lots, too. A real family.

Welcome in, I said to these creditors.

I understand, I said to the men.

Okay then. Thank you!

We don't really have a head for these things. We're writers. We'll pay for everything now. I mean tomorrow. When we can.

Thank you for stopping by and for going to the trouble!

Have a good day. Thank you. Thank you.

I closed the door behind them and we laughed. Mom's ugly table that we'd lugged down. They can take that and maybe the cabinet, you said.

No, not the cabinet, it has always been in my life and in the family long before that, too. A few years later that cabinet would be in your study, steeped in smoke, like the table, which had also belonged to my mother.

Why did you furnish your study with my mother's furniture?

Our children would look back on the Mauritius trip as the best trip. Turtles and eels at their feet when they walked in the water. The endless zoo and the warm atmosphere. The violet evenings and the dark nights. It should have gone on like that forever.

Had this memory come up first because it was harmless? I don't know. I told Maria I wanted to go home right away and she told me such thoughts were pointless. You'll stay here, in peace and quiet, and be sluiced out when you're done. When I protested and shouted and crashed into some poor unsuspecting patient, I was given another shot and the last thing I saw before I went under was Sister Maria's face bent over mine. She was whispering to me. I beg you, don't remember more than you can handle.

I took a break from the memories. Anyway, how could I know what I remembered and what I had forgotten? Not here. I'd have to get out into the real world to know. Several months later I was standing in the auditorium at the children's school listening to a lecture on the importance of reading for a child's imagination and for their future well-being. When the lecture was finished and we parents were supposed to go to our children's classrooms where the parent-teacher meeting was to continue, I suddenly had no idea where I was. We had three children in that school, and as I was supposed to be deciding which child's classroom to visit, I realized that I had no idea which classrooms were my children's or who their teachers were. I stood still as the room emptied out and when everybody had gone I went up to the principal and asked where our son's classroom was. She showed me, without revealing that she thought there was anything strange about the question.

But this was much later. For now I was wandering up and down the hospital corridors and I still remembered nothing of what happened after the summer. Well, except the air ambulance. Are you sure? No. Maybe not. What was it I said? Yes, I remember. The motor's sound, the men, the mattress. I lay there, strapped down, and there was an echo. The years in the countryside, those I can't account for either. I remember the children and that you were in your study, I remember writing and the few occasions on which we had visitors. I remember you paying for the house like a gangster.

*

I remember the staff in the ward because I'd seen them so often before. There had to be an end to it. This has to be the last time. Otherwise they'll keep treating me and treating me with electricity until one day I'll be just like the stone woman in the corridor. The woman I'd seen during my very first visit to a ward like this, back when I was young and didn't understand any part of what was happening to me. That woman could frighten me at any hour of any day. I would have gladly forgotten her, but she was stuck in my mind, like a nightmare that won't loosen its grip.

She was a patient. An older woman who

sat still on a chair the whole day long. The color of her face. The gray skin. How she sat there like a living mountain, breathing. But her eyes weren't alive. Were unmoving. A white, cloudy membrane covered them and everyone who saw her understood she was the living dead.

They tried to wake her up with electricity. As I said, I was young then and my easily frightened mind would gallop away at the slightest notion. I tried not to look when they rolled her out on the gurney after the shock therapy. I couldn't imagine the horror she'd suffered through. Electricity to the head! They passed the rec room where we were sitting around doing nothing or else devoting ourselves to our torments, and my entire body sensed that our being able to see her like this, utterly defenseless, wasn't right. We who witnessed her journey from the factory into our ward knew something about her that she didn't know herself. She was as big as a whale and barely fit on the cot, and it took four care workers to drive her that long stretch into her room where they would use their collective strength to roll her onto the bed.

Her body under the yellow hospital blanket. I despaired over her being transported like this. There she was on display. Deep in sleep, unaware. It wasn't right. This I knew.

For many years I myself would be transported in the same way, in the deepest sleep, for all to see, and I didn't think it was as bad. Why? I don't know. I tried to imagine myself laid out on a gurney in full view, but now there were so many of us following the same path out of the factory that it wasn't an unusual occurrence. We were used to it.

The doctors who tell you the treatment is working, but that they don't know exactly why. They point to the patient's instant relief. To what appears to be euphoria and is interpreted as the patient having been cured of their illness.

If electricity is so damn beneficial why is electroconvulsive therapy banned in certain countries? In a number of states in America, in Holland and in Germany electroconvulsive therapy is hardly used at all, and in Italy it's banned.

I'll move there, maybe I'll finally be safe.

It's in the Nordic and Anglo-Saxon countries that the treatment is commended.

Those fundamentally different ways of looking at a person. Her human worth. Her soul. Her memories.

Electroconvulsive therapy was first used in 1938 by an Italian psychiatrist who got the idea from a slaughterhouse. He watched as worried pigs were calmed by electric shocks. I know, he says, we'll apply this to the weakest among us. Those who can't speak for themselves.

Researchers who are against electricity say the euphoria is actually a symptom of brain damage. This is challenged by other researchers. On this battlefield electricity stands as the clear victor. At least in my part of the world.

Are the brain cells destroyed, as many say, or are they actually regenerating faster, as claimed by others? The manic brain's cells are renewed at lightning speed and are particularly sensitive to electricity. This the devils know. Neurologists suggest both the former and the latter, regeneration and destruction, and nobody knows its impact on an individual level. Those who are most critical of the process describe electroconvulsive therapy as a neurological catastrophe.

Therein lies the conflict.

On the other hand everyone agrees that it has a severe impact on the memory. Everyone.

I didn't know this then. The information I had was the information I've already mentioned. The treatment is gentle. It can be compared to restarting a computer. It takes a lot of strength to resist the doctors, and there wasn't much of that strength in this ward. And they don't need the consent of those involuntarily committed, which I was. They could go right ahead. A table decked out for you Mondays, Wednesdays, Fridays.

In the whole wide world, the country of Sweden conducts the most electroconvulsive therapy per capita.

What I'm going to say next is important: Don't be afraid. Everything I've truly feared has come to pass. So I'm telling you: Don't be afraid. I've often wondered what freedom is and I've come to the conclusion that freedom demands responsibility, self-respect, and a calm, warm heart.

I could have stopped here, but I'm driving us on a bit farther, or as far as we both want to go. You can exit this story anytime you like and that's what makes this arrangement so rare. I want to say one more thing. Take care of your dreams. Some say there's nothing more boring than hearing others talk about their dreams, and whenever someone says this I wonder, How can you and I be so different?

There is nothing more exciting than when someone, preferably someone close to me, tells me about a dream. To have access to their unmediated fantasies, in which nothing resembles the reality we live in, but which can nonetheless cast light on the place where he or she now is.

Sometimes dreams can determine a life choice without your actually being aware of them doing so. Here's a dream I dreamt the night before I decided to become an author. I was in despair. My dreams of acting had bottomed out. I would never do theater again. I'd made a serious promise to myself, the kind you keep. Once again I hadn't been accepted into that coveted acting school. I was told I wasn't good at collaborating and I ransacked myself on the night train up to the beautiful but chilly city where I was living. When had I not been collaborative? Had it been during the final exam?

I searched my memories and found it.

As we were reading the script we were later to perform I thought we were doing too much reading.

We have to get up on the floor, I said. Otherwise we'll still be sitting here with our scripts when it's time to perform the scene for the jury.

Right as a jury member walked through the door to check in on us, I'd said, Can we stop whispering?

Was this the reason?

Surely it was that Polish chief physician, I mean teacher, the great pedagogue with whom I rode the elevator up to the sixth floor. He looked me in the eye and said:

You're afraid is what I think.

In the evening on my way to bed I broke up with the boyfriend I was living with at the time and who had so kindly picked me up at the train station because he knew me and knew how destroyed I was. I asked him to leave the apartment right away. Then I fell asleep and dreamed this dream.

It was summer and I was staying on two adjoining islands in the archipelago. I'd found myself inhabiting such a pleasant existence, where I never hesitated about anything, not about what I was going to do next, nor about whether or not what I'd done so far was good enough. I rode the small ferry that traveled between the islands. Because the trip took no more than a few minutes it was with an unworried ease that I hopped from one island to the next. I spoke with others without fear, and the summer vacation seemed endless. But as always happens whenever you spend too long in a state of bliss, peace became panic. Suddenly he was back—my dead father was standing in front of me alive and well and only a few years older than myself. I stared at his fat stomach, looked into his green eyes, and with a single gesture he demonstrated his dominion over the island. He waved his arm above the crowds, which suddenly closed up behind

him, and I knew my life was over. His mocking. Finally he was the great man he'd always
dreamed of being. He was the leader of the
island. I quickly glanced at the bridge, no
ferry was waiting. And why I was allowed to
stand there on my own, I don't know. Maybe
because I still couldn't get myself anywhere.
I looked at the water. After a while something emerged like a creature from the deep.

A black locomotive rose up and the train
carriages became the tail of the beast. The
engine appeared and flashed in the sun, then
dove back down into the depths. The only
way to get off the island where my father
reigned was by that train. A train that frightened me to the core, but instead of throwing
myself into the water and swimming to
those black carriages and somehow getting
myself out of there, I thought about painting a picture to memorialize the sight of the
black engine rising out of the waters and
showing itself. So I ended up staying on the
island where my father would torment me
for all eternity. When I woke up late that
afternoon the mail had already been deliv-
ered and on the doormat lay my acceptance

letter to the writing program I'd forgotten I had applied to.

At least I got into that one damn school.

It must be said that suddenly something felt good. I believed in destiny and, in spite of it all, I felt so relieved that I was going to be able to devote myself to a pursuit I was actually interested in and so it began. After a year and a half on the island I'd finished my first book. It was as though I'd written it in my sleep, and this truly frightened me because it didn't feel as if I knew what I was doing when I was writing. This feeling has never left me, though perhaps I have grown somewhat used to it.

I know I'm incapable of resisting when my interior calls upon me to act. For several years I had been so in love with a man across the Atlantic that I didn't know how I was supposed to go on living after he'd beckoned me only to then dump me as though I were worthless. In a letter he informed me that he did want to stay in touch, and what was cheering inside me as I read the letter was a joy that couldn't be contained, so when he wrote a few weeks later *Being with you is a bet no one could recommend*, I ended up in a limbo where I remained for many years and where I perhaps still am. He was the one who first put words to the weakness that a year or so later would be given a name at the factory. I was like a homeless person, I couldn't find my footing, and in my fantasies I wanted once and for all to show him his mistake, that I was perfectly normal, balanced; but I never succeeded. Instead I wrote confused and revealing letters to him, which only worsened my position. He built a family with children and I did too, and I swore to all that is high and holy that I would never contact him again, and yet I did. We exchanged pictures of our children and I sent him the first book of mine translated into English and didn't hear a word. When my husband left me it occurred to me that I should have shown the translation to him instead. I should have shown my husband that I was fully present with him and the children who I was so close to that I could sense the slightest shift in their faces and bodies and yet I regularly betrayed them by leaving. How could I choose the factory over my loved ones? What was I looking for in those corridors when everything I wanted was already in my home, in the family I finally had for the first time in my life. Why did I flee my loved ones? Who knows how paths cross? How do you stop and let everything wash over you in the place you most want to be? Dependency and freedom can coexist. You can't get love on its own.

I feel my thighs under my skirt as I walk. I just might be getting out of here.

It's a regular day. Aalif is helping an old woman get up. He calls her My Lady.

The place I fantasized about being had ice skaters on the lake, a thermos of coffee, oranges. The icebreakers I waved off in Stockholm reappeared in Luleå. How do you endure? You grieve. Start again. Count the steps. The snow had been on the ground for months. You tossed my morning gift to me as if I were a dog. Was this the first sign? This day tastes of iron. We know we are alone. The children come, one by one. Nothing bad should ever be allowed to happen to them. Their hands out in the sky. We were plucking the stars. Washing dishes. We ate of each other. Our dreams mourned their origin. We forgot in order to make space. Were we afraid of death? Yes, but we were more afraid of life.

I am tired. Tired of everything. I can't see through the window for all the mosquitoes.

Where is the key to the weapon cabinet? I sleep away my life. Zahid gives me medicine. Apparently the electricity isn't enough. My usual lousy medications, which gave me a full body rash and dried me out, did more harm than good. A hyperactive thyroid then boils. Later on I traveled to the Lofoten literature festival with a boil on one butt cheek, which made it impossible for me to sit down. An extraordinary place, Lofoten. The crystal-clear water. The bright nights and the high mountains. As beguiling as it was treacherous. In Västerbotten, where my father was born and raised, my illness was called the sunshine sickness.

You should have stayed there, Dad. You know I'm right.

The curtain flutters. And yet not a window is open. Of course not a single window is open.

Are you there? I often saw my father in passersby, in a crowd, on the train. Sometimes he was everywhere. Have I been too harsh with you, Dad? I don't know, Linda. Have you been harsh? Did I frighten you while I was alive? What do you think? Do you remember when we were alone in the apartment and I went to bed at five in the afternoon just to get away from you. You asked me the same thing then: Are you afraid of me? No. I'm tired, Dad, that's all.

Zahid zips through the corridors and the pattering of his light-blue plastic shoes can be heard at a distance. He looks at me and asks how I am. Instead of answering I ask him how he is and he smiles and says he's nervous about going to his brother's wedding in Afghanistan. I ask if he'd rather stay at home and he responds, Yes, but, you know. Suddenly I feel like a child who can't muster the energy to do her homework, can't muster the energy to shape her future, and I say I'm sorry. Zahid laughs and says:

I'm guessing there are lots of people you should say sorry to, but I'm not one of them.

He waits until I've swallowed the pills, and

pushes his cart onward after saying See you tomorrow morning. I'm already sweating over how much it's going to hurt when he inserts the needle.

Once I woke up after the treatment with one enlarged pupil and the other a tiny speck. This made the factory worry. It deviated from expectations, and I was sent for a brain scan. I looked at myself in the mirror and Sister Maria was standing next to me, solemnly saying that there was a risk it might stay like that forever. What did it matter to me? I didn't care about my pupils. I might as well have one light-shy pupil and one that let everything in. Bipolar pupils. Might as well, so it would be clear what sort of person I was.

In any case, poor Zahid was supposed to insert the big needle and he was even more frightened than usual and put it in wrong, spraying us both with blood. He apologized and I said it didn't matter to me. He was so stressed as he wiped us off, pale-faced, saying we were going to have to do it again. Mistakes aren't allowed in the factory. There were so few carers and nurses working in the ward. Instead of making his second attempt with the big needle, he really should have been handing out the medications, which were waiting in their boxes, numbered to match the doors to our rooms. This is why he stuck the needle in as if it were a matter of life and death, and to his relief it was a bull's-eye. Then I was transported down a few floors to be met by a doctor with a non-regulation-length beard who laid me down on a stretcher.

I hope you're not claustrophobic, he said, looking at my pupils and shaking his head, as if to demonstrate just how badly they had messed up. A little while later I slid into a long pipe where my brain was photographed. Once back in the ward, I asked to see the photo, but the electricity doctors were holding on to it and the event was forgotten as quickly as it had begun. A few days later my pupils were back to normal and the treatment could be resumed.

Again I sat in the waiting room with Aalif and I asked if he was bored. He said he was never bored. I got up, but he gently pulled me back down to the bench, laughing as usual, and said, Everything is fine. Under control. Under control.

The memory exercises Maria did with me were of her own invention. The time she spent asking me if I remembered where I grew up as a child or what happened the day after my husband said he wanted a divorce, she'd saved up by inserting needles faster than anyone else and, as I mentioned before, without the patients feeling a thing. Maria had grown up in Austria and she spoke about her homeland as if it were heaven on earth with its fresh air and the undulating, green landscape. And what authors we have, she whispered to me, and I could only agree with her. Maria's caring for me was quite remarkable because she could attach electrodes faster than anyone else in the factory.

She asked me to write and said it was my way out, but the words wouldn't come when I sat down in my room with the paper she'd given me. Maria didn't like that I had lost my memory, I could tell, and, as I said, she did what she could to bring it back. The children, she said. Think about the children. I started crying whenever I pictured them and she thought this was a very good sign. Don't avoid what is hardest, she said sternly. Cowards don't get anywhere. And stop feeling sorry for yourself.

The next morning it was my turn to visit the chief physician, Charlotta said. Charlotta had a slight limp and when patients asked her to buy things from the outside, she couldn't refuse. Chocolate, cigarettes, postcards, and stamps: she'd buy them all if you gave her the money, well otherwise too, that's how nice she was, and she knew when to hand out her gifts, or what she'd been given money to buy, so that no one noticed. She was retiring soon. No one knew exactly when, and worry followed her wherever she went. Would she be there the next day or not? I'd never asked her to buy anything. I shivered at the thought of smoking a cigarette, but had I been offered one I would've taken it. When I lived with you I almost kept pace with your smoking. Once a day I went over to your writing shed and smoked a cigarette and we exchanged a few words, even though you didn't like to be disturbed. But if I didn't disturb you, we wouldn't speak at all, and even though I knew that was what you wanted, it was not what I wanted.

*

I always worked myself up before doctor visits. In the few minutes you had at your disposal it really was hard to get a word in. The chief physician would do the talking, making sure the patient left the room knowing only as much as when he or she had walked in. But this time I had a concrete question to ask, in addition to wanting to appear optimistic and sensible to avoid being prescribed another round of treatments. Impossible, but I'd try anyway. My situation couldn't get any worse. The thing was, lately and all of a sudden, I could suffer an ... I'll call it an attack because I can't find a better word. Suddenly I'd feel a giant's foot pressing down on my chest and I wouldn't be able to breathe. It happened several times a day and was particularly intense when I was trying to fall asleep in bed. Getting up and walking around the room helped a bit, and so I'd barely had any sleep, which made me feel both fearful and weak.

I kept repeating the question I'd prepared in advance until I was sitting in front of him, whoever he was. He was new, as the doctors always were, and he started the conversation by saying that he'd studied my case, plowed through each file starting with the very first time I'd set foot in the hospital. How ambitious of you, I said encouragingly, and then fired off my question. The one about why I was suddenly unable to breathe and would feel like I couldn't endure. He looked at me and asked when I'd last felt that way and I replied honestly. Right as I was about to enter his office. Without thinking, he suggested I try square breathing. Hugging ice is another effective technique, he said, would I like him to order bags of ice for the ward? I said, No thank you, I'd rather do square breathing. I plucked up my courage and said that, in the short term, I understood the wisdom of diverting your thoughts to get rid of the feeling of not being able to breathe, and continued by saying that the method of replacing one pain with another wasn't going to get to the bottom of why I suddenly couldn't breathe, and this applied to all human suffering, of course—this needing to understand the reason for the torment that makes life feel so unlivable—and why do you advocate electroconvulsive therapy when all that happens is that I forget everything important to me, but then our time was up and the chief physician asked me to leave the room, as he noted in my files that I was to continue the treatment.

Sleeping got harder and harder, but not because of the giant's foot on my chest, and when I felt the breathlessness coming I took the doctor's advice and did square breathing until it passed. No, it was more like the sleeping pills weren't working and without them I was wide awake. My restlessness increased and I asked for stronger sleeping pills myself, but as soon as the thoughts stopped wandering through my weary head and sleep was within reach, just as I was mercifully drifting into dreams, I would wake with a start. This cycle repeated itself all night long and I was quickly transformed into a shadow. My under-eye circles were as dark as coal. I, who'd always eaten large portions and helped myself to seconds and thirds, even when it was hospital food, suddenly couldn't eat. The hunger that had been driving me on through the days disappeared at once and all I did was lie in bed. I was wasting away, and in the end only Maria dared force me out into the corridors in an attempt to tire me out. After a few days, I was a wreck. I couldn't calm my thoughts, which were running loose with a previously unknown power and madness. Consequently, the treatment was paused.

One morning as I lay in my room staring at the wall Maria came in. She practically screamed at me to stop moping around like some old sad sack. I'll say it again, she said once she'd gotten a hold of herself, there's no reason to feel sorry for you. I'm not about to stand here and remind you of all you have, what a privileged person you are, but try to send your thoughts in that direction. This apathy is ridiculous. You're degrading yourself. Get some part of you to prove that you want to get out of here. As she said these words in my dreadful room, I leapt out of bed. I would never hit Maria, this I knew, but I wanted to scare her while she was shouting about responsibility and duty.

Instead of hitting her I shouted back: How was I supposed to get out of here if she kept sticking electrodes to my head and chest every other day? We heard steps in the corridor. Loud noises were unacceptable and I assumed Maria would blame everything on me, but when three care workers entered the room, she told them she was giving a certain spoiled individual a dressing-down. After this scolding I wasn't tired anymore. She'd managed to wake me up and I was ashamed because everything she'd screamed about me was true.

I walked out into the corridor and asked Zahid, who was on his way to the office, what it would take to get out of here. He glanced at me and quickly replied that he had no idea. He was just a nurse.

I don't remember how I replied, or how I got to bed that night. By this point I was afraid of my dreams.

Good morning, said Zahid. I'm going to insert the needle now.

His hand was shaking, and to calm him a bit I changed the subject. I asked if he was going to go to Afghanistan and, while patting the back of my hand, he told me he was leaving early the next morning. How long will you be gone? I asked. Two weeks. Will your whole family be there? Yes, well, no, my mother isn't going. She doesn't have the energy, Zahid said, and pricked the vein in my hand. I tried not to show how much it hurt. But it's her son's wedding, I continued, after Zahid had secured the cannula with a bandage so everything was in place and flushed through the needle. Once you entered the factory there was such a rush that the cannula for the anesthesia needed to already be in place. They didn't have time to insert needles. There are some things I don't talk about, Zahid said, making a quick exit. Maria's voice echoed in my head. You're spoiled. You can't play the stubborn teenager anymore, you're an adult with many children. You're supposed to be at home caring for them, not living your life in here where nothing means anything to you. I got up and ran into the corridor to apologize to Zahid, but he was nowhere to be seen. A care worker whose name I never learned caught me and asked me to return to my room. The treatment isn't until ten o'clock. You can sleep for another few hours, he said and escorted me to my room. I was furious with myself. I wrenched my arm from his grip, saying I could walk on my own. I shouldn't have. I made lots of these mistakes. I had to behave impeccably for them to stop the treatments one day and open the door to the world from which I shrank. A world I'd never chosen, really.

Did I want that? I asked myself. Yes, of course. Would I want to stay here? I don't know. You're acting strange. I know; I'll stop. No more outbursts, I promise. I'm not going to do anything. The day they have nothing more to say about me is the day they'll release me. Yes, and what will you do once you've been released? There's nothing you want to go back to. The house. Imagine walking in there. From the hall, what does the interior look like? You're not clear about anything. You sit down on the sofa and then what? I'm going to see the children. We're going to live in the house together. Yes, yes. What will you tell them when they come to you? It has been a long time. You know so little about yourself. I've always been close to them. Still, you took a big risk by setting foot in the factory. You've been here many times. What do you get out of wandering these corridors? What do you get out of the treatment?

I stood by my bed in the room, and the care worker whose name I never remembered pushed me onto it. He chuckled and left.

What I don't understand is why they persist when the only result is that I lose my memory. Maybe they have to keep going until I can't remember any of their names or actions. I'll forget my name and where I've been. I'll forget the factory.

There's a knock at my door and Aalif peeks in. Three minutes, he says, and I wonder what I'm supposed to do in these three minutes. Orient myself? Prepare for those few steps into the factory? I wait out the time until he knocks again. Time to go, My Lady, Aalif says and smiles. A yellow hospital blanket is hung over his arm, the blanket that will keep me from freezing when I'm asleep. I get up and leave the door to the room open. I walk next to Aalif. If I were to deviate I'd be intercepted. If I were to run away from Aalif and disappear into an elevator, the elevator would stop. Within a few seconds of the alarm sounding, four, six, seven, ten care workers would appear. They'd run in from the nearby wards. The first time I deviated Muhammed was first on the scene. Have I told you about Muhammed? He looked so disappointed, like I'd truly made him sad. He was prodding me along to keep me going in the right direction. If you deviate you get intercepted. The treatment can't be fled.

I walked those twenty steps to the factory. My mind blew things out of proportion and I steeled myself. Like a person awaiting death. Was this what I was hoping for? The narcotics inevitably carry a small risk. The anesthesiologists are aware of it. They're very thorough, but still patients have died when under. I don't know if it has happened here specifically, but I know there's a risk. As they ask their questions—if you've eaten or had anything to drink that day, if you have any loose teeth—my blood pressure is measured and because mine is so low they ask if I tend to faint when I stand up and I say what I always say: I have never once fainted. I could've said anything, but the authority of the anesthesiologists is such that you, remarkably, want to do your very best, and being a person who doesn't faint is better than being a person who does faint. How strange that they don't recognize me. By now they should know I'm not someone who faints but, each time, they look at me like they've never seen me before. The anesthesiologists nod at the student at the ready with oxygen and while I take deep breaths of the gas as requested I sometimes think the anesthesia won't put me under and that they're going to turn on the electricity while I'm still awake. I take a deep breath and imagine the pain and, right as I'm about to take off the oxygen mask to ask the anesthesiologist a question, they inject the anesthesia and its cold black shadow darkens all consciousness so they can serve me up to the electricity doctor, who doesn't hesitate to flip the switch.

I wonder what moves inside me as I lie beside the other sleepers, if I feel unease. Can it be possible not to be at all affected by the crowds gathered behind the heavy drapery? Each sleeper must be able to sense the proximity of the others on their beds. Maybe we think our siblings are lying beside us, but that deep narcotic sleep makes you incapable of turning over so as to avoid touching anyone else. You sleep this forced sleep and in the dreams you dream those who are forever wandering your mind are in motion, but in a way that drives you further and further into the room that must belong to death. You witness your burial, and as you're about to be lowered into the earth you find yourself on a freshly scrubbed plastic floor.

A nurse enters the room to which you've somehow been taken. You've been pushed into bed or have climbed off the gurney yourself, still asleep before the scream you scream finally wakes you. You don't know where you are. Where are you? Why don't you recognize anything? The fear upon waking—until, finally, fully conscious, you realize that what you've woken up to is far worse than your dreams.

You never get used to the treatment. The dreams you dreamed were muted at first, but after a few confused hours you'd wake from them with the scream heard so often in this ward nearest to the factory.

You would wake up like a newborn into

life. Who were your parents? Who would teach you to live the life you'd been given? *No one* was the answer. No one would teach you. Here you lived no one's life and nothing more was expected of you.

When I was small, there weren't many people I wanted to be like. Even though I studied my mother carefully, I never wanted to be like her. Instinct told me we had nothing in common. From early on, I knew I needed a mission. I was a child, and had nothing against being one, but I wanted to do something real, not just grow up and go to school. In the countryside, I spent time with a girl who was four years older than I was, Therese, who taught me all the dances she'd learned at what she called show school. I was proud that she was so much older than I was, but she didn't want to tell me what it was like to be alive and to be so old. I was allowed to be around her because I did everything she asked of me. We may have been codependent: she on my services and I on her praise. I knew what to do when I was with Therese. That was all there was to it.

I didn't have an unhappy childhood. Neither was it a happy one. It was no one's childhood. I didn't know who I wanted to be and this made me weak. I longed for something to show itself to me, and you could say that one day it did.

We had gone out to the archipelago with Mom's friends.

They were radicals. Engaged lefties. My mother was never honest about herself. She was adaptable and offered everyone sweet, happy smiles, which was appreciated. She had lots of friends. She marched on behalf of women's rights, of course, but she wasn't really engaged. Not like the other women. It's not like she had the time. Her time went into the theater, into keeping me and my brother close to her, and into parrying my father's actions. She had a full schedule.

Those damned politics were on the menu, in any case. Those people seemed to speak with their entire selves and I didn't know what I was supposed to do when the daughter of the family approached me. She was much taller than I was so she leaned over me, pulled me aside, and said, They play guitar and smoke marijuana once the children have gone to bed. She pointed at the greenhouse. That's where they grow it, she said. She looked me in the eye, waiting for me to respond. When I didn't she said it was illegal. That the police could come and take her parents away.

Something happened that night. After dinner we were supposed to go out on the boat. Who wanted to come along? I shot up my hand and said I did. I don't know why, maybe it had to do with the strange mood and with their daughter Daniella, who I'd sneak looks at when she wasn't looking at me? Anders, who was Daniella's dad, laughed and said that hand-raising was unnecessary here, and I immediately apologized. This bothered Mom, who gave a hacking laugh, high yet low. But sweetie, she said, and gestured to everyone around the table, these are all nice people. Everything was left on the table and Anders waved his napkin to indicate that one thing was ending and another was about to begin. He grabbed the guitar, which was leaning in a white basket chair, and started to sing. Everyone sang along, even Daniella. The song was in another language, a language I recognized but didn't know from where. I squeezed my eyes shut and tried to get to the place where I'd heard that language, yet found nothing where I was looking. Maybe because I was searching the wrong landscape, with other people. The song was familiar somehow, its sound. It felt close, like an action performed so often it had become automatic. Whenever Mom sang it made me uncomfortable because I didn't think that she could. On top of that, she was pretending to be political. It troubled me that everything was so different.

I walked behind the others on the road, kicking rocks. I tried to get the stones to crash into each other and fly apart; in the best case, it sounded like a gunshot. I used to rub the stones together for so long they'd act like magnets do when you try to make the negative sides touch. There was power between them. They wanted to stay together, but nonetheless avoided each other. It didn't last long, only a second, but I liked the sensation, how the air between the stones was charged with a power I couldn't name; maybe

I could relate. Desiring closeness, but being unable to have it.

Our large group walked down to the water. I didn't know if it was day or night. I heard my mother's voice up front. Everyone was laughing, shouting to each other and I thought two things. One: They had enough on their hands. Two: I would be the one to row the boat. I wasn't good at much, but I could row. This thought was so intense everyone should have been able to hear it.

The water was quiet. Gray and smooth. I'd always liked boat rides; my entire being knew this delight. And I loved lakes. I never wanted to go in the sea. I didn't like the openness, looking out over the horizon. I can't tell you how I knew, but I knew I liked lakes that tasted of iron. I liked lakes, wooden docks, water lilies, and pond skaters—how they could walk on the water like Jesus, the rings around their legs. Maybe more than anything.

It was clear I wasn't going to see any here; this wasn't fresh water. What is water called that isn't salt, isn't fresh, but is weak and characterless? I don't know, but what happened next was that Daniella and I were both sitting by the oars. She sat down a second after I did and should have known the impetus was on her to move, but she stayed put, her eyes blank. I tried to say something, but found no words. My head, my whole body, was on fire. Finally I stood up in the boat and declared my intention to row on my own.

First, the boat fell silent. I don't know what happened, whether they looked at me, or at each other. I heard my mother's anxious high laugh. Daniella's dad started to say things like, Can't you row together, each take an oar? The boat is pretty heavy. I just stood there in the hull, feeling the burning behind my eyes and in my wrists. Mom wobbled over to me and tried to stroke my hair. What's the matter? The longer I stood there, the more nervous she became. It's not a big deal, is it? We're going out on the lake. Her ingratiating tone when she asked me to sit down. It's only a little outing. I could feel everybody's eyes on me but I couldn't sit down, not now it had gone this far. Why don't you take turns? Anders continued. You go first. I didn't look at anyone. I started counting out loud to hold back the tears that would squeeze through as soon as my voice wasn't loud and clear. I knew this, like you know night follows day, and because I didn't want to say anything I counted. I was counting as loud as I could, and once I'd started I couldn't stop. I counted louder and louder to vanquish the tears threatening to streak my face. I wished I could disappear, I wished I hadn't stood up in the boat, but now I couldn't sit back down. Humiliation was everywhere. In the air I breathed, my thoughts, which were praying for a miracle. What was I to do now? The ache behind my eyes forced everything else out. I knew the tears would win and I would lose. I couldn't keep breaking the silence with my counting, and when the tears finally started to run down my face, I jumped out of the boat. It wasn't deep so I waded to land and ran back to the road. I ran with all my might in my wet shoes and clothes. I knew they weren't going to follow me. Mom would say something about letting her be and then they'd row out in the boat and I wouldn't be there so they couldn't talk to me. I knew I'd destroyed something but I didn't care. I didn't care about anything, not about my dumb tears, not about my fear.

I didn't know what I was supposed to do once I was back at the house with the outdoor furniture and all those plates and glasses. I headed for the outhouse. I locked the door and immediately felt a sort of relief. I sat down on the toilet lid and cried until there were no more tears. All fell silent. I mulled over the incident and concluded that I was appalling. I wasn't a little child who could simply be excused, nor was I grown. I was somebody I didn't want to be: far too childish in my thoughts to be turning ten, yet at the same time my solemnity stood in the way like a wall. I wasn't a likable child; I never smiled, I didn't answer questions, I was full of demanding feelings, I didn't know anything and yet I thought I knew more than everybody else. My fantasies were grand, I was going to be a pop star, I wrote poems on a wrinkled piece of paper I kept clutched in my hand like a weapon. I longed for someone to read them, not Mom, I couldn't care less about her, but someone else, someone I dreamed up and planned to run away with. I tried to imagine what he or she would look like, but I couldn't picture anything. I imagined the person who'd see my poems and like them would be my real dad. I dreamed intensely about a different father.

Once my mother was in a relationship with a man called Tom. He lived in an old house in a part of town where I'd never been. He had his own horse. He rode several times a week. I liked what he looked like when he was off to the stables. Riding boots, brown full-seat breeches, a riding jacket that smelled of horse. In fact, the whole hall smelled of horse. I did everything I could to make sure Mom and Tom could be together as often as possible. I noticed my mother wanted this, too. Tom spoke to me not like I was a grown-up, but as if I were an equal. He didn't understand why my mother would speak to me so thoughtlessly or superficially, and sometimes he'd argue with her about that. About how she was as a mom to me and my brother. Mom, who had a hot temper when it came to her children and how she was raising them, asked him not to stick his nose in. The children were her business. I often sat in the tall grass in Tom's wild-grown garden, listening to them fight. A window would be open, or they'd be having coffee outside. You don't have any children, she'd scream. You don't know what it's like. Who are you to tell me what to do with my children? They're my children. I sat there hoping Mom would die so we could move in with Tom.

Secretly, I wished my brother would die too, of an incurable illness, so we could all mourn his death, and me and Tom would get to live alone.

Once the lot of us followed the road that led downhill and had an Italian ice cream on Mariatorget. The ice cream tasted so good; we were all happy, relaxed, and giddy. I don't know why. I hoped it was because I was going to get a little sister. I'd often thought my whole position in the family would have been stronger had I been the eldest rather than the youngest. It would be me and her.

But the two of them didn't say anything concrete, nothing of value. It was just a nice atmosphere, and, for me, the feeling of being abroad. The ice cream really was good. I wanted to go back there every night and nagged and nagged Mom. It was summer and the theater was closed. She didn't have any summer engagements, any excuses; we were together and I was happy. I knew that this was what I was. I liked Tom so much that I asked if I could accompany him to the stables. I don't remember why I wasn't allowed to, I don't remember everything, but I remember the sense of security. The garden. Mariatorget. Maybe he was the one who'd said no, but I don't want to believe that. Not after the way he talked to me. As an equal in his care, but an equal nonetheless. Me being a child and Tom being a grown-up was never made an issue, still I'd never felt more like a child than when I was with him. I concluded that riding was his domain. He wanted to ride his horse in peace. Maybe it was his way of being alone with his thoughts about him and Mom, who didn't want any more children, to ponder if loving her was possible since she never let him have a say when it counted. Dad had been in the hospital for a long time and he wasn't about to come out either. He refused to take his medicine, he refused psychological help—even when Professor Johan Cullberg himself offered therapy, which of course my mother had arranged. He didn't want to be healthy. He wanted to live at Beckomberga forever, he'd tell anyone who could be bothered to listen. Fixed mealtimes and care, even if it was strictly professional. Ward 86 was his arena. There he'd organize chess tournaments, which he'd always win, and would lie about his fantastic life and how wronged he had been. But away with him and his weakness and his way of taking over your life. He who dragged prostitutes home to my mother's apartment when she wasn't there and then turned on the gas. Away with him. Let him rot out there in the corridors. All there was to do was start this new life with Tom as my dad, which he also wanted, right up until the morning my brother threw a knife at him over breakfast. I froze in my chair, terrified, but gathered myself quickly and thought that now they'll see what my brother is like, a violent devil forever angling for a fight. What happened instead was my mother started laughing. She laughed and stroked my brother's cheek as though she and my brother were the couple and not she and Tom. Then Mom squirted fermented milk at Tom. Mom was like that. She was absolutely impossible.

Tom got up and walked off, and there we sat, my mother, my brother, and me at the soiled breakfast table and everything was as usual. The dream I had been living shattered there and then. Tom understood that my mother would never let him into this Bermuda triangle of ours where everything foundered and went to hell. I never dared ask Tom if I could live with him or told him I couldn't keep living with my mother and my brother after having tasted paradise. A real family. I tried to scream, but it was like in a nightmare where the sound won't come out. No one heard me. I screamed and screamed without managing to get any sound out. Tom didn't come back. I knew I had to fight harder than ever before. I needed to solve this situation that Mom was laughing off, but I didn't dare. Did you hear that? I didn't dare. I had never felt as happy as I did with Tom. I wanted to move into his old house. I wanted him to have custody of me. Tom would protect me from my father. More than that. He would become my father.

Mom and Tom split up that day. I heard it loud and clear. I lay under the steps and heard his calm voice say, It has to be the two of us. You and I are the adults. Your son can't rule over us. You can't defend him when he throws knives at me. You have to set a boundary. He can be as angry as he likes, but he's not allowed to throw knives at me and now that he's done it you can't simply laugh it off as if it were nothing. Why are you afraid of telling your son off? He's eleven years old. You're his mother. Be his mother. He's asking for it. He can't be allowed to rule over you. Over us. Do you understand? I am not a mean person. I want the best for you all. I want to live with you all. Are you sure you and the kids don't need some sort of help? There's no order to anything. Your son thinks he's the man of the house and your daughter never says what's on her mind. Have you noticed? She only says what she thinks will make things easier for you, and in between she has those outbursts. I'm worried about her.

Here, however scared to death I was about everything being destroyed, I fully enjoyed hearing Tom talk about me. About Me. About me and how he thought I was doing. This last fight may have been when I understood that I needed to stop all my nonsense and become a child that was easy to like. I had to become as wild as my mother. As strong as she was—but superior because I was going to be as clever as Tom.

Many years later when I asked Mom to tell me about Tom she said breezily, It never would've worked between us in the long run. Then she added this, which had the same sting even though I was grown and should've understood: I wasn't that in love with Tom. It wasn't as serious as you think.

The outhouse smelled sweet, of decaying wood and sun. I decided to leave everything behind. The boat. The company. My way of starting something and getting ensnared in my own dumb actions, which nobody cared about anyway. The irritating habit of taking an action past the point of no return. I looked through the little window over the meadow. I thought, If I see a deer, then everything will be fine again. I looked and looked out the window. Tall grass and some flowers. All was silent and I was about to start counting aloud again but stopped myself. I tired of looking and took the newspaper on top of the pile by the wooden wall, but as I was flipping through it I worried that the deer would appear when I wasn't looking, so I glanced outside. I wasn't reading the newspaper, I was looking between the pictures and the window. After about an hour I lost interest in the deer, which might or might not turn up and then vanish. What did I care about a deer? Screw it.

I flipped and flipped through the old sunbleached newspaper. When I heard voices nearing I suddenly saw a photo of a girl and wondered if the photo was of me, we were so alike. I managed to read the little there was about this girl before I quickly lay down on the wooden floor and pretended to be asleep.

My trick for escaping unbearable situations.

Only the bad memories made themselves known. I would've gladly forgotten my childhood days, but it was like they'd been etched into my cerebral cortex. Out of the electricity's reach. I convinced myself of a lot of things. Certain things I knew nothing about. Like how to behave in a romantic relationship, how to shape your life and to benefit from knowledge. I had learned nothing. There were good periods and bad periods. The bad ones had increased and increased and the good ones lessened and lessened. Before I'd been a whiz at standing tall, but now I was living my life stooped over. I tried to flee in every possible way. I didn't want to know myself. All my mistakes lined up before my eyes as soon as I paused and thought clearly. Having been so close to my children when they were small didn't matter, even if I hoped that their earliest childhood was stored in them for the future like a seedbed, because what they remembered most was that I was a mother who could disappear. I wasn't only hurting myself, like when I was young; I was also hurting my children each time I left them to stay in these rooms, these corridors. Not to mention how much I had hurt them before, serving up my bad judgment for breakfast, lunch, and dinner, weeks in bed, in a room that could get as hot as fifty degrees centigrade in the summer. In that room, my thoughts boiled and became a mass of quashed sorrow. There, far too close to their wondering bodies, their worried gazes and growth, I wasn't their mother anymore but someone else, someone they feared and didn't understand. I frightened them. I frightened my children.

I was somewhere. In dreams I could catch sight of myself and the road I would take.

I was in another time with the children in a beautiful old apartment, which must've been the one I'd lived in as a child. I knew that apartment better than anything else. I was there and small wooden beds filled the living room. There all the children lay asleep, dreaming of the life I would show them. There were so very many of them and I was just one person. Soon they'd all wake up at the same time and I'd start running around with food and clothing and they became more and more and they were so lovely, every single one, and I photographed them in the evenings as they sat on the floor watching TV. There were big things happening in the world, but even bigger things happening in their hearts and imaginations and I knew I couldn't do anything but look at them intently enough to etch their dreams into their DNA and into my worried hands. I was theirs and they were becoming more and more and I was surprised by how beautiful they were when they laughed, I opened the door for them and they walked down the stairs and over the street into the park, and the park was full of them, as if they'd gathered before a demonstration, and they were marching out of my dream and when I woke up it was to tell them something, but as usual I had no voice. I fell out of bed and Maria helped me up and told me it had been a good seizure, a successful treatment, and you should sleep a little more. A little more. A little more. Sleep a little more. Sleep and never wake again.

You're going to die. If you don't die, you'll almost die and never die for real. You'll lose everything important to you. You've already lost it. You are all alone.

Have I said that I lived in a crappy city in a house I could not stand? It doesn't matter, but that's where I was to return. I had bought some furniture. Thrown in a few things at random. Nothing I dreamed of was possible. I had no one to talk to in that little city. No friends. I looked down at the ground so no one would see me. My hatred for that place was so strong I could have thrown the city into the sea had I only channeled the sum of my hate instead of wasting it. The beaches eroded a little year after year. The wind was constant. I refuse to speak that little city's name.

Back to the outhouse on that long-ago night. In one of the newspapers I saw a picture of a girl in a camp in a rural Soviet village. The way she was looking beyond the frame of the picture immediately roused my interest. She was one of several, but still all alone. She looked exactly like I would've wanted to look had I been able to figure anything out. Braids, the blue rosettes, a knotted red scarf, white shirt, blue skirt, the red star on her chest. She was a little Octobrist and had distinguished herself by speaking in front of the other little Octobrists and the somewhat older pioneers in the camp about the importance of carrying the Soviet spirit in your entire being. By keeping what was best for the Soviet Union in mind you could let everything else go. You didn't have to be a child anymore. You were already a comrade.

Little Octobrist, I thought. Pioneer. I would look like her and join the collective. This was what I discovered that night, after I'd decided not to care about the deer who might or might not turn up in the meadow and before I lay down on the floor and pretended to sleep. I would transform. I had seen myself in the picture.

I didn't immerse myself in the Soviet Union or communism and yet at once I became like them. It suited me. I had been born an October child. I was a chosen child among other chosen children, but I'd gone off track in a way no human could understand and that's why they were calling for me everywhere. Their voices were what I heard when I woke up in the mornings.

For several years I wore a pioneer uniform. It made Mom uncomfortable, and she found it hard to explain, but I knew who I was and this fortified me. I was no longer so maddeningly vague. I was no longer weak. This may have contributed to my loneliness in those first years because I was at an upper-class school. The children didn't know what my uniform meant but some of the parents said I was a communist child and it didn't take long before all of the children started calling me "the communist." Whenever anyone asked me if I was a communist, I'd say the same thing: No, I wasn't a communist. I was a pioneer. They were two different things. I had borrowed a form that could simply be slipped on. Form leads to freedom. This was my lesson in those years and I've continued to benefit from it. I switched out my family and lived my life as part of a collective that didn't exist, but no matter. This life was more real than the one before.

I learned nothing as a child. Not in school and not in my early adult life either. I roved the corridors of my imagination to find nothing much was happening in there either. I didn't listen to music, or try to find myself. I did not lead a youthful life. I went to the stables twice a week and I read books. My head was empty and I didn't give a thought to my body. I was certain and yet was nobody. In my rather meager fantasies I was one girl among many. There were no parents, no boys, and we spent a lot of time hiking in the mountains to other small villages and inaugurating various military parades. I lived in another time with myself. When I sat in school solving problems in my math book I was a different girl doing the same thing but in a classroom the other members of the collective sought out. Everything could be replaced. I was consumed with going first, farthest, and not stopping to rest. Which is why, in reality, I spent my afternoons walking through the city's every neighborhood. Not having a boyfriend or engaging in schemes was crucial, so I didn't take an interest in anyone and thought this was to my great advantage. No one could take anything away from me. I had created someone else who I preferred. A person tougher than I was. Tougher and stronger. An indefatigable person with qualities entirely different to mine. This went on for as many years as I needed her. This girl is perhaps my most remarkable creation and I have never felt the desire to explain to myself what I was doing in those years that I was her.

She had her life under control, for which I was grateful. Even when I stopped wearing the uniform, I still carried it inside me. I had access to her whenever I wanted. Maybe I still do.

I entered puberty late, so I was a child much longer than I care to admit. I smoked in the subway during recess when I was thirteen, before my body started to change, but I still played in a way that belonged to childhood. I couldn't stop reading certain children's books. I had them memorized and anyway they gave me much more than the grown-up books I read. I was late growing into that new body which I had no interest in discovering. I started to become extroverted and incautious and I didn't like myself. I took the sudden crushes that arrived out of the blue and raged inside me as a sign of weakness. So as not to lose myself in my love for my friend's older brother who I couldn't have, I coupled up with his friend Erik. He impressed me with his many talents. He had won the Swedish championship in fencing; he had been allowed to skip a grade because he was so gifted in school. He was especially good at mathematics, which I thought of as a language I couldn't understand at all, though I admired those who could. I remember that my friend's older brother talked about the time Erik was asked if he could solve the equation on the board—no one else had been able to figure it out. Erik tried, but even he couldn't, and the teacher had asked him to sit back down, looked at him sadly and said, *Et tu, Brute*. Even you, my Brutus. I don't know why I still remember that, probably because it made a strong impression on me. Being so talented in a subject you were interested in was a big deal. Admirable.

There was a certain age difference that was a little difficult to handle back then. When he graduated from high school I was about to leave ninth grade. Like I said, he'd skipped a year, so really it was like he was at the end of eleventh grade. Was he only two years older than I was? That's not right, he was so much more grown up, more mature.

I think Erik was mindful of the age difference in a way that didn't encumber me.

When he one morning in the house in Vallentuna said he loved me, something seriously changed. Erik was in love with me. With me.

A few hours later, in the cemetery below the church in which we'd celebrated so many graduations, I sat smoking and repeating these words for hours after school. In love. This was big. Important. Meaningful. I was just as in love with him. Suddenly life was serious.

We started taking pictures together and we developed them in his bathroom. I liked taking pictures of him. I overexposed the images, rendering him almost invisible, contours and light. I thought the photographs were beautiful. He was easy to be with. Open, maybe. He gave shape to my new life as a young teen and made it possible to keep all that came tumbling down contained. My dad, who otherwise didn't care what I did, met him a few times and afterwards he'd always say the same thing: Never leave him, you'll never find anyone better.

Of course this was irritating. I broke up with him after a year and a half. I think I'd hidden myself with him to keep my anxiety in check, and it had almost worked.

The anxiety was unleashed in my life when Euro-railing the summer after ninth grade. Surely it had been there the whole time, but now it had a shape and was taking over my life. My friends and I smoked hash on the French Atlantic coast one night and I've never recovered from that night. Suddenly I was running through the small city trying to find the boarding house, at the same time it felt like waves were finding their way inside me, rolling down from my head, through my body, and back up to my head, where they'd break against my forehead. I ran around the city searching and when I'd found my way and had opened the door and lay alone on the bed in my room, the currents were raging with such force that it didn't matter if I was clinging to the bed frame, and nor did it stop when Nina came home and I asked her to lay on top of me. It was a onetime thing, but this somewhat bold act of daft rebellion cut open a path in me that made way for the anxiety to walk right in. After that, as soon as I experienced any form of worry, every time I was afraid of going through it all again, the feeling returned. Again and again, whenever and wherever. The waves breaking against my head. I can still feel it inside me when I get afraid. The pull, the power of which is as frightening as a feeling of detonation behind my forehead. How it can't be resisted. I think the violent worry I experienced then was what made me so afraid of being alone. Then and now and in between. The worry diminished me, made me cowardly and ingratiating. I adapted myself to the reality I lived in in a previously unimaginable way. I refused to be alone. I avoided myself like you might avoid somebody you don't want to run into in the hallway at school. I went out with scrawny boys from my high school and could often hear my father's words ringing. Never leave him. How could I have left Erik for these upper-class idiots? Not that those relationships were long-lasting, on the contrary, but they were embarrassing from start to finish. My friend Nina was going out with one of them, too; I wouldn't call him an idiot exactly, but whatever. Nina was unusually gifted in math, and one day as she was helping her maybe not entirely embarrassing boyfriend with his math homework, his mother came into the room where they were sitting and said straightaway:

Coco, are you letting *a girl* help you?

It was at that level. I weathered a number of harsh words after Swedish Lit when the teacher read my essay aloud, or when I as usual was the only one who wanted to comment on what some poem or other might possibly be saying, or on what similes were. *Roses in a vase that's cracked are roses nonetheless.* How could you translate the image into something else? They couldn't figure that one out.

Essays were all I actually really cared about and I'd get so nervous before an essay, as if my entire existence hung in the balance.

Maybe it did. Maybe it was the only time I refused to adapt, and I nagged our teacher to grade the essays in time. He never did.

Being good at school was of the utmost importance, and triumph was allowed.

In my class, the students' last names dripped with old money, and with this came the self-confidence that old money affords and the knowledge that life would turn out well for them. You could see in their posture, in the way they walked, that they had nothing to fear. Maybe I envied their self-confidence, their way of crossing the schoolyard, how they took a seat on a chair in the classroom and immediately owned the room they were sitting in. Even the teachers sensed it and some admired them. Our history teacher Rolf Rendel in particular. He loved to address students by their last names. What year was the Battle of Lützen? Young Mr. Adelswärd? How did the French Revolution begin? Von Halle? Leijonhuvud? Fredrik Gyldenstolpe? They always knew the answers. I did my homework for the most part, but my interest in history was not piqued and I never managed to bring all the various epochs to life for myself and sometimes I didn't know the answer when Rolf Rendel directed his questions at me. He loved France and French history. The Versailles Peace Treaty, how did it come to be? Miss Boström? Christ, did I really need to sit there and take shit from that loser? But I didn't say anything. Well, one time I did.

The first term, while I was still with Erik, I had a lot of absences. My mother was touring every hole in Sweden with an inane play called *Afternoon Market*. She had to speak in a Smålandish dialect and she really wasn't good at dialects, so from start to finish watching her was embarrassing. At least I was living alone in the apartment. Luckily my dad was in the hospital, otherwise he might've turned up. He didn't. But he did call. He'd set his mind on having a fatherly chat. A chat he had yet to have because mother had prevented it, or so he said. He was manic and couldn't be stopped. Suddenly, he had so much to say to me.

You're like Andrej.

Andrej was my brother's best friend and a model student. He was especially gifted in mathematics and went to a special math-focused high school with several languages as electives, and he learned Russian in no time at all. He could speak six languages. To be fair, he'd gotten three on the house. Swedish, Spanish, and French, but he quickly learned Russian and Italian, on top of English. He used to visit us on Sundays when I was in middle school in order to help me with my math homework.

I protested to my father and said, Of course I'm not like Andrej. Andrej is a wunderkind. Of course I'm not like him.

But Dad was unstoppable. He went on about how talented I was, only so he could conclude that all of my traits came from him. Your mother, he said with dead seriousness, hasn't left a mark on you. It's all from me.

I don't think so, I said. I'm not like either of you, and you're starting with this now? You who haven't given me a single birthday present since the divorce, you who don't help Mom with the upkeep even though your disability pension is sky-high. Compare your disability pension to her salary, *and* she supports us and works all the time and you're an abyss that can't handle anything and that's all I know of you and I am over the moon when you're hospitalized, because it's the only time I can be sure you won't be coming here and forcing your way in, destroying everything, as usual. I hope they never let you out, and, of course, you do too, so we're in agreement there. Can you just hang up and never call me again?

I only said those superficial things that were easy to say, nothing real, because I didn't dare. It always ended the same. He'd cry and say, I'm the world's loneliest person. When he was manic he'd speak in his Norr-landish dialect, the first sign that he was on the upswing. After some months, he'd leave his bed, start singing songs, speaking Norr-landish, and then he'd go out and blow a lot of cash and it was all pretty innocent, but when he was living at home I had a constant stomachache and kept out of his way. I never went home. I'd sleep at other people's houses, lying to them about having permission to do so. I wandered between my friends' homes because, even after the divorce, my parents had an agreement that Dad was allowed to live with us, even if Mom was living with other men and he was there when they were. It must've been so humiliating to see Mom with other men in the apartment and it didn't end once he'd gotten his own apartment, because he would come to ours during his good spells and cook dinner and play cards with us and bake buns. It was insufferable, even if I enjoyed the buns, but we didn't say anything to Mom. Why? I don't know, but we didn't. Or maybe my brother did, because in the end this ended too and we were home alone when Mom was at the theater. Well, not completely alone, we had live-in nannies who were students, but I didn't want to be with them. It felt like I was alone and, in our family, feelings were of considerable importance.

Dad went on about how his mother had died when he was thirteen and how he'd taken care of his younger siblings all on his own. He'd studied to become an engineer at night school and commuted twenty kilometers by ski each day.

I know, Dad. You've told me a hundred times.

Still, this last detail never failed to impress me.

Then came the obligatory: Your mother destroyed everything when she said she wanted a divorce. We used to be a nice family, he said, crying.

I never mentioned him stalking us and almost gassing us to death and hitting Mom and terrorizing us. I didn't say a word about what he'd done to me when I was little and alone with him and my brother in the country because that was something I couldn't tell anyone. I don't even know if my brother remembers. He was the one who put a stop to it. My dad had a certain respect for my brother.

Your mother is a whore; he was working himself up.

You're the whore, I finally said when I ran out of fucks to give. You're the one who ran around with prostitutes and let them wear Mom's clothes when we were out of town, so you tell me, so who here is the whore, exactly?

He hated being contradicted and would come up with stuff like:

What has happened to you? Don't you

know how hard it is for me? Nobody visits me. Nobody.

In the end I was the one who had to hang up and pull out the jack, which was annoying because how was I supposed to know if anyone else was calling, someone important, maybe Nina's older brother, who I was in love with even though I was with his best friend. Unfortunately it is possible to be in love with two people at once. My love for Erik was always clear, present, and calm; my love for Magnus simmered and then would suddenly blaze up, causing me despair and unhappiness.

Or what about Nina, my best friend, whose friendship made me feel guilty because maybe the reason I was at her place so often was so I could increase my chances of running into Magnus. It was humiliating because we always played cards, fucking Bismarck, which my dad also loved to play and which I'd always lose at because I wasn't smart in that way and not being intelligent mattered to Magnus.

I was alone in the apartment and couldn't cook, so I ate crispbread sandwiches with cheese and all it took was for me to think about something for too long and my worry would manifest and so I'd have to call someone who would let me come over and this sapped me of all my energy. I was so plagued by worry and the sensation of waves rolling through me. Erik didn't understand what I was doing, because I refused to tell him why I was turning up at his place and acting so strange: Can't you just take it easy? I skipped so much school my homeroom teacher finally called a meeting. He said the teaching staff was concerned about me, his words, and if I didn't attend every lesson from now up till Christmas he couldn't give me my end-of-term grades. That's a shame, I replied, because I'm about to take a week-long trip to Egypt with my boyfriend.

Of course you *can*, my homeroom teacher responded. But you can't go now!

I swear I won't have any absences next term. That's a promise. But I'm just going to take this trip first.

Are you on drugs? he asked, and I despaired because of course I wasn't! Or was I? I did smoke hash that one time and I felt so guilty about it. Could he tell? Was it obvious that I was on the slide? I stayed in bed and writhed in sweat in the mornings and only came to school to eat lunch and then left again. I sat in cafés and wrote. Quite often I went to a café where a certain young writer spent her days writing in a large black notebook and smoking. She was always there and I admired her violently and read all her books when they came out, thinking about how I had seen her. I had seen her writing this book. Or I'd just walk around town during the day because it soothed me and dispelled my worry. In class I fell behind and hadn't done the reading and couldn't follow and didn't know anyone. Drugs? Was it because I walked around with a large, battered brown leather jacket and had dyed my hair red? Did I look like a druggie?

What makes you think that? I said.

You're never here. We're worried about you. We keep trying to call your mother, but there's no answer.

I'll ask her to call you, I said. And I'm not on drugs! I've never done drugs! Is that what you think? Give me my end-of-term grade, whatever it is. Next term, I'm going to show you all.

I went home, called Erik, and vented. Okay, he said, Come over. And I did, but it didn't help, not like it usually did.

A few days later we packed our suitcases and flew to Cairo. Erik made sure we fit everything in. He walked around with a map, finding his way everywhere, and I tagged along. He was so organized and beautiful and I just fell into his way of being. Interested. Direct. Ambitious. We saw the pyramids, went to all museums. We walked the streets of Cairo and the feeling of being alive was so wonderful that I told him I loved him and he said he loved me, too. Deep down inside I really did feel that I loved him. That life with him was real life and that my life at home and in school was a garbage life. We took a taxi to the Suez Canal and Erik grilled the taxi driver. Where did his family live? How incredible was it to live in a country with such a rich history and how did they build the Suez Canal? How were they able to stop the sea? Did a lot of people die? He was interested in architecture. I mean, really interested. The taxi driver leaned on his horn the whole time, while telling us about everything we were passing by. Neighborhoods, cafés, half-built buildings. Everyone driving a car in Cairo leaned on the horn and all that noise woke us up early in the morning in our dirty hotel room, which we both found exciting, but Erik did most of the talking and he told me about what he was seeing and experiencing and I wondered why I wasn't experiencing Cairo as intensely as he was. For me, it was more about the feeling of being away together. In a place where nothing was like the life I was living otherwise. Why wasn't my experience of the pyramids as intense? My favorite part had been riding those weary dromedaries through the desert. Erik had gone along with it for my sake, but, because it was for tourists, it wasn't as valuable as exploring Cairo itself.

What I remember most from that trip is standing by the Suez Canal and watching the large ships pass through the channel where Europe meets the Red Sea. Two continents so close to each other. A feeling of something larger than life. That this was the big wide world. It was windy and the wind was so hot and the amount of sand flying around in the air made it almost impossible to see and the sky was white, not white with clouds, but white in and of itself. The taxi driver talked and talked and suddenly he turned to me and said:

What a nice boyfriend you have. You must be a good girlfriend to have such a nice boyfriend.

Why wasn't I a nice girlfriend? What did he know about me? Nothing. I thought that I had to get my thoughts out somehow. I couldn't just live my life inside myself. We flew home and the next day I broke up with Erik. I was going to transform myself and he didn't fit into my transformation. I was going to be a student at the Östra Real school. I was going to attend every class, even if I was sick, which I never really was. I would shore up my life and put an end to my muddled ways.

Breaking up with Erik was a terrible experience. He was so good in every way and he would never understand why I suddenly didn't want to be with him. I'd spent the day gathering strength. I would just get it over and done with and then go to my hair appointment. I was going to dye my hair dark brown and then cut a bob. I was so nervous sitting there in the window and looking out over the park. When he rang the doorbell I steeled myself and ran to open the door. In his arms was a bouquet of pale roses. They were the loveliest flowers I'd ever seen. I didn't say thank you, I didn't say anything. I just went to my room, Erik followed; I placed the roses on the bed and turned around and said I'm breaking up with you. Erik didn't believe me.

So the flowers were overkill, I get it, but you don't have to take it like that, he said.

Oh, but I do, I said. It's over between us.

What? he said. Why are you saying that?

I'm saying it's over between us.

Stop it, Erik said, still smiling at me because he thought I was just feeling anxious or whatever. He wasn't taking me seriously, in any case.

I refused to explain. I didn't know what to

say. It was just a strong feeling I had—I needed to sort myself out and he couldn't be in my life while I did. Or maybe it was because I was nobody when I was with him. Or maybe, most of all, because Magnus had said that I'd outgrow him. I made him leave and got my hair cut and it gave me a brand-new look and I started studying and I attended all my classes and it was out with the old and my mother returned from tour and everything was normal. Everything was sort of good again. I didn't worry. I found a way not to. If I felt it coming, I'd shift my focus to something else. To what I was reading, or to my appearance. I decided to start wearing makeup and be good at school, maybe not the best, but really good. I would be better than good at the things I was good at and I would make an effort with everything else. Only math was a washout, but I got lucky there because our teacher was an alcoholic. His line was: The teaching staff is hunting me down with a blowtorch. He was often absent and couldn't really teach and he knew it, so I got a middling grade out of guilt. In all the other subjects I made up for my quite terrible start, and doesn't everybody love a comeback kid? The teachers were happy. My grades shot up that second term.

My mother tormented me by saying things like how she missed Erik, how she didn't understand why I'd left him. One time she really rubbed it in, saying, I saw Erik in town. He looked so sad.

Of course I wanted to call Erik. But. Now I was actually feeling better. I was a different person. My homeroom teacher asking if I was doing drugs had been such an earth-shaking experience that I delighted in straightening out each question mark. I didn't dress like the other girls. I didn't wear a red Canada Goose jacket or any of those things, but I don't think I stuck out. That's why it came as a shock when my social studies teacher, the centrist swine, humiliated me in front of the whole class one day. I mean, that square Gert Lienhart was an active member in the centrist party. He ran up and down the stairwells before the election talking with people about the benefits of a centrist politics, and he piled on his centrist bullshit in the classroom, too. Throughout the entirety of high school he never once mentioned our assassinated social democratic prime minister, Olof Palme.

He began his tests the same way for three years. Who was Margaret Thatcher? He found this amusing; she was his idol. You were supposed to answer *prime minister, Tory, Great Britain*. Lienhart hadn't forgotten that I'd had no idea who Margaret Thatcher was on the first test, so one day when I couldn't answer another question, I don't remember which, he didn't let me off. Think. Think. You really don't know the answer? I guess I got angry and said, No, I don't know the answer to your question. What he said next I'll never forget: You spend your nights in the center of town between Sergels Torg and the Royal Dramatic Theater, don't you?

I fell into a shock. My temples were throbbing. What was he trying to say? That I was buying drugs on Sergels Torg? Everyone else laughed. What an ass. Still, I had no comeback. I just sat there and took it. To this day, it bothers me that I didn't straight-out ask him what he'd been implying.

That scumbag Lienhart knew he'd crossed

a line and ended the lesson. I told Mom what he'd said and she got so angry that she called him every night at six for three months straight. His wife was the one who'd answer. No, I'm sorry, Gert isn't home today either. I didn't need to lift a finger to end up with the highest grade for my remaining years. Never again did I answer his question about Margaret Thatcher.

Those were our teachers: cholerics, alcoholics, idiots.

This is why Lena Ragne, the philosophy teacher we had in the third year, stood out. The boys hated her, called her a fucking cunt because you couldn't study for her tests, you had to demonstrate your understanding. Which "ism" suggests that in twenty years we'll be able to make the unhappy happy? No, they couldn't figure that one out and it made me happy. Lena Ragne passed around a list of terms before the test, and those you could memorize in half an hour. The rest was comprehension. Funnily, even the parents put pressure on her, saying things at parent-teacher meetings like:

Look at Putte's other grades. Are you going

to be the only one who gives him anything but the highest grade?

I still think about her lesson on existentialism sometimes. She asked us to stop taking notes, saying: I'm about to tell you something you'll never forget. People define themselves through their actions. Actions and non-actions; it's not just what you do, but also—and perhaps even to a higher degree—what you don't do that shapes you as a person. You are your own ethics. You are doomed to freedom.

How did I end up there? Among Östra Real's hallways and these upper-class dummies? Well, because I became a dummy, too. I felt ashamed by how much and in which ways I had adapted. Here I was somehow fitting in, while secretly insisting I was someone else. There I was in a jacuzzi in Djursholm with some random girls and gross guys I didn't know who were watching a porno while ashing their cigarettes in the churning water. I hit my limit. How low can you sink?

In those years I lived parallel lives. One life, not like an upper-class girl's—you can't fake that, it's in the spine and embedded in the DNA—but, still, like that of someone who'd adapted to the unwritten rules of Östra Real. I kept my politics to myself, and never mentioned that I was a Social Democrat during those years.

I think my mother's work as an actress at the Royal Dramatic Theater was exotic in exactly the right way. There were a lot of upper-class parents who'd go to the theater just to drink champagne in the marble foyer during intermission. I think Mom's shine rubbed off on me. I was accepted. How the hell did that serve me? It got worse when I started going out with one of them. Not Oskar, he was nice, and we weren't really together anyway, but Greger, who I was with for a week during graduation time. Imagine him compared to Erik! Everything I had experienced with Erik and everything I had not experienced with him. We were both grateful when it ended. I decided not to be with anyone and he got back with his ex, relieved. My tough side also did its part to ensure that I, not quite unscathed but still anxiety- and worry-free, emerged from the darkest three years of my life with good grades. Grades I never put to use. Both of my Swedish grades were enough to get me into the independent university courses I would later apply to. What a relief it was the day I finished. But what would I do with all my freedom?

I was drunk on alcohol and joy and in the evening I ducked out of my own boring graduation reception to go to Nina's house to meet Magnus and everyone else who was there. Which included Nina, of course; she was my greatest comfort. She was always kind to me. I wanted to go to that new club Hunky Dory, but I'd also wanted to leave early because I didn't want to get wasted and fall apart, but I was also afraid of walking home alone in the dark. I mean, who might I run into? Anyone could attack me, or drag me into a car, and Nina was understanding about it all because she knew me inside and out, so she said she'd walk me home and then go back to the club and it excited me to hear the door slam shut around three, four in the morning, and then Nina would have to give me the play-by-play, who'd said what to whom, before falling asleep, and I'd lie awake digesting it all. I'd be up all night after Hunky Dory, even though I never drank more than three beers, never spirits. By this point I knew how to drink so as not to make a fool of myself, or behave in a way that would make Magnus think less of me. Hunky Dory wasn't a place where my classmates and their kind went. We only got in because a distant relative of Nina's had founded the club. Nina and Magnus were, as luck would have it, not upper class, but in my eyes they were whip smart and, in their home, serious discussions were had about exciting things and their mother often sat with us, which I liked, but I liked it even more when Magnus paid attention to me. Sometimes he would, if he was in the mood. I was so in love with Magnus. Even his bumping into me when he passed by set off the feeling of an elevator being ridden inside me. I was more in love with him than I had been with Erik. Stupid, I know, but that's how it was. Magnus, who never in his life would be with me, still meant more to me than anyone else, and at his and Nina's house I could drop the Östra

Real act, but that didn't make it any less exasperating as the things I thought I'd mastered weren't what counted there. We never talked about literature, never about theater, which in a way was liberating, but still. I tended to be quiet when we were all together. Only when we drank could I set my shyness aside and join in the conversation.

Still I appreciated the shyness and caution that arose in me when I was with them as much as I enjoyed letting these feelings go. Dropping my shyness like a garment that slides right off you and connecting in a deeper way, more important, more meaningful.

My shyness was more authentic than the mouthy persona I'd adopted at Östra Real. At least I was being real when I was with them. That's how I was. In their home, I resembled myself in the way you resemble yourself when you're not lying, in disguise, or building up a front so fragile that the slightest breeze would leave you standing in a corridor naked and defenseless. I abandoned myself so easily, and for what? To spend my years at Östra Real as if I were a somebody?

Someone who dazzled with their knowledge of literature, understood every poem, but still couldn't spell *integrity*.

Why do I torture myself with memories from those years? What is it that's still not resolved, over and done with? I mean, what distances haven't I traveled since then? All young people do violence to themselves. Growing up is not child's play.

I've written that sentence before. Repeated sentences are irritating. Or, are they the most important ones?

Maybe I shouldn't have taken things this far, but how far did I take them, really? I kept to myself and that new dark bob of hair was still me. But then there was my severity, my fear of losing track of what was important and, possibly worse, the feeling that I, even though I hadn't bullied anyone, had still been part of defining the status quo. Who was in and who was out.

What use is this to me now? In these outskirts, where I cling to my torments so as to keep from seeing something even worse. The loneliness, the feeling of no longer being loved, of not being able to love. My children call to me in my dreams and here I am up to my elbows in shit. I who no longer have an embrace to take cover in, alone, without anyone to hold on to, conquered by life—and who'd wielded the ax? Him or me or no one at all? Was it I who fled my life, or was there something I wasn't hearing, yet was nonetheless drawn to, and which spoke to me in a different voice, a clearer voice, and which with clear eyes was watching me walk in the wind and, out of fear, retreat to those familiar outskirts of the soul. The soft nightshirts, the set mealtimes, the bed, the bed, the bed.

Wake up. I command you. Wake up!

Depression's torpid darkness, its void and waking death, it's what awaits me when I sink deeper. To where there are no words, no consciousness, just dull slumber, morning, noon, and night, the anxiety enveloping every cell.

Each morning when you wake up, the fear when you finally realize, with every part of you and with every thought. You are awake.

So many mornings I've woken up thinking, feeling that everything is as usual. The house, the children, the husband who has only gotten up in order to work.

I thought we were written in the stars, he and I. I said as much when you asked for a divorce. It has been ages since you've acted as if we were written in the stars, you said, and then we took the car and drove it into the landscape and we talked and it was early summer, everything was in bloom, and in the midst of it all, the feeling that now, right now, the walls were crumbling around me. And yet in the midst of this awareness of life and death there was a joy over connecting with you. We spoke, and it had been ages since you'd spoken to me in that way. Like you wanted something from me. It was the two of us for the very last time.

I've since wondered about that joy. What had I experienced there in the car? An intense recollection of life, both outside in the spring, in the colors, and with us in the car. The feeling was akin to speaking too slowly, like being underwater, or both near and far. The words reverberated. An intense sort of pressure, yet everything was clear. I wasn't afraid, not then, it was as though I could carry everything. Yes, exactly. I can carry everything. Everything. I am not afraid of anything.

I have always held myself in high esteem. No one needed to tell me I was good at writing. I knew it deep down, even in the years I wasn't writing: All I would have to do was sit down and the words would come. I knew like you know you'd be capable of killing a person in battle. Give me the knife. I'll kill you. If it comes down to you versus me, know I will emerge victorious whatever the fight. Maybe my dad's words are what led me to believe I could handle anything. Anything at all. No, they were my words that I used on myself when my vision was clear. Sometimes I'd fantasize about war just to know how it felt to be invincible. Presumably a result of my genetic predisposition to delusions of grandeur which blossoms every now and then.

I've always known I can write as though it were a matter of life or death.

It is a matter of life or death. But life isn't meaningless when I'm not writing, the writing lives inside of me, I'm just waiting for battle and my capacity to work is such that it feels like all of me is singing. It's so easy. I follow the flow of words and nothing goes wrong. If it does, I sense it right away. Anxiety strikes and I'll happily throw fifty pages away if they have led me astray. Usually the words lead me right. I know I should be incredibly thankful. I don't care what others might think and I rarely take advice. I might need your thoughts, when I'm unsure of something or feel ashamed of what I've written, and in our years together you put a lot of wind in my sails. You knew me so well you could tell what I wanted to achieve after only a few pages and you'd fling out a word knowing it would be important to me if I ever got stuck. You'd tell me to write instead of moping around and wasting my time and I'd tell myself that, too, because I listened to my own voice most of all. I appreciated your perfect pitch, but enjoyed mine more. It felt like letting all the horses run free. As if I were sitting high up on a buggy and driving into the night, still surrounded by light. I knew the horses were in the stables, waiting for me. They were kicking the walls, full and bored, when I entered the stables. Until finally you would arrive. The horses were wide awake when I hitched them to the wagon, the strongest closest to me, the skittish ones up front, so the reliable ones would support them; the moody horses could see best in the dark. All there was to do was take a seat in the coach box and let the horses run loose like in one of Mauritz Stiller's silent films. Selma's horses galloping in *Gösta Berlings Saga*. No, they were my horses. Mine alone. With horses like these, you couldn't drive off the road. All of them black. It was a joy. It was freedom. Freedom.

As a child I loved it when we rode out, when we'd gotten a good ways into the forest and would let the horses gallop. That feeling. Not like when they bolted. It was pure happiness. The powers that were unleashed. Being one with the horse, rising up and out of the saddle and leaning forward and letting go. The horses loved it, too. What happened in the forest was like a secret. We never talked about it. We'd remark on how it had been a good gallop and such, but what we didn't talk about was the feeling of strength in those minutes we decided to give it our all.

Taking the reins and galloping together, then stopping and letting the horses walk home, reins slack, was also a good feeling. On the inside you know how long you can let go and just enjoy the speed and the freedom, and when it is time to stop. It's almost better than writing. Galloping with open rein through the forest.

At riding camp we were allowed to swim with the horses. We charged into the water bareback. When the horses started to swim, we'd slide off and hold tight to their necks. Some riders got a hoof to the leg, the horses just swam, giving no thought to us, but I was never kicked while in the water. My body was relaxed and glided along. Like now.

Did I protest? I could've refused. Refused to go to the factory.

Not then, when I couldn't speak for myself. Then I couldn't have done anything.

But later? Why didn't I? Didn't I care? Well yes, I did. But there was no way out, so I just went along with it. Got out of bed when it was time and walked those twenty meters straight. It couldn't be said that I didn't need the treatment. It never helped me. It did the opposite.

No one listened.

I couldn't make any decisions for myself as long as I was here against my will and was a danger to myself and others. Those were the rules. People who didn't know me wrote about me in journals, which found their way into the hands of every new doctor I met. The law around involuntary treatment. Distorted perceptions of reality. Mood swings. Speech latency of over a minute. Possible administration of Haldol.

Restrictions. Were there more? Yes, something could always be corrected, added, regulated. The highest charge of electricity. Less electricity gave fewer side effects, but it wasn't considered as effective.

How could I be there week after week without anything beginning or anything ending? Who was deciding over my life? Why had I capitulated and who was holding the strings?

There were no answers. No precise, actual answers, so I would settle for scraps from the

table of the engorged. I vouch for, well, everything they ask me to, about three hundred
trips up and down the corridors. They ask
me to walk. They offer this corridor and I
don't complain.

I can't find my way anywhere. I haven't
even learned the simplest of things.

Do I want to die?

I don't know. Even this I'm not clear on.
Really dying. Who knows if there's anything
on the other side? Imagine if I have to repeat
my same mistakes for all eternity? I can
think of no worse hell. Who cares about life?
Everyone. Everyone cares about life. Hold it
dear, like in the fairy tale. Why not? Let's do
it for the sake of my enemies. I get up. I take a
step out into the corridor.

After all my mistakes I've learned to think
of life as a duty. Children are born, one after
another. I was put into the world to take care
of them. I know that. Forgetting this insight
has cost me. Far too much. It will never happen again.

Medicated patients crowd on the sofas.
They pretend to watch TV, a debate of some
sort.

I move on, cross paths with a doctor on my way home. It's the worst of them all. Alexander. I decide to look right through him. His heart is beating fast in there. Is he afraid of me? Aalif and Zahid see me pass by. What am I doing? Sleepwalking, maybe.

Who are you, the knights of darkness? Who among you dares set foot on these treacherous grounds? Come inside, where everything dissolves and disappears. Don't weigh down your dejection with sorrow. Shed what you can and take a step towards the factory. That state of bliss. Neither light nor dark. Dreams that wake you with a shriek. Yes, you remember. Their tiny bodies. The particular joy of birthing them.

I was in love with our newborn baby and couldn't stop looking at her. The enchanting time when I was hers and she was mine. Anna is hungry for knowledge and brave. She can wander the earth's paths and never falter. She can do what you could not. Walk straight ahead. All of your children can. They belong to themselves, as you do when you've never met with danger. Why am I lying? So we all can sleep and stop dreaming that endless dream. It's not needed anymore. You've always been such a pessimist. Directionless somehow, with tears in your hands. Wipe them away like everyone else does. Get up. That's right. What do you see?

I see Zahid handing out medicine. He is dressed in white and wearing those light-blueish and minty-green plastic shoes. Do you see anything else? Well, yes, in my dreams. So dream. Dream. If only it were so. These days find their end. Someone takes my life and vanishes with it. Okay. We're giving it everything we've got. You see us at the far end of the corridor. It's true, there aren't many of us. But you're strong, aren't you? We are your dearest wishes. Really? You tire us out as though we were your lovers. Put the fire out. Let the water spread. We are all sinking. It's simple. Stop breathing. Stop being who you are. Okay, I'll obey, why not?

*

Speak clearly, like your mother taught you. It's not hard, in spite of the meds. We sat in the window in the hall and I learned to speak with that tone of hers. What were you talking about? We were speaking clearly to each other about sunsets and how straight the school corridors were. They led me straight through my childhood. All you had to do was walk straight ahead and fall to your knees wrapped in a white shroud. I remember telling my confirmation priest, to his horror, that I had taken communion even though I wasn't baptized. I'd read the letter thoroughly. It didn't say anything about being baptized. Three services and one communion. That was all it said in the documents I'd received. I have almost always been prepared. Nobody told me you had to be baptized.

Confirmation camp was all my idea. I found my own way to the Graninge diocese. Two weeks later my brother was sitting in church, arms crossed, and my mother was reluctantly giving me a gold cross at the reception afterwards and, in protest, *Vogue's Body and Beauty Book*. It rained for two weeks at camp. It was like deliverance leaving that place. I'm sorry, God, but it was. The confirmation priest immediately pounced on my mother and confessed that she wanted to open her arms in a more sensual way. Could Mom be of assistance? Mom tried not to laugh, and kept her composure as usual. Maybe Mom was street smart. She made everyone happy without leaving so much as a crumb behind. She really did show that priest how to open her arms to the congregation, but she did it with a sort of smile that I knew meant she was only pretending. This escaped the priest, Mom laughing behind her back.

I traveled home with my mother and brother. My brother didn't say a word the whole trip, still it was good to be home. They reproached me for all the fuss with the confirmation and God, and it was a relief to fall into Mom's arms. There, there, you're home now, Mom said, stroking my back. This was a mistake, she said. You don't really believe in God, do you? No, I don't, I said, and then we laughed it all off and went to the movies.

Is there nothing that you enjoy remembering? Some instance from your youth or early adult life that you remember with pride?

Maria's voice, a voice I was used to hearing. Maybe we were related? I don't know what I think about Maria. Why is she always here? It's unpleasant. She's like something out of a horror movie. A small pious woman who has suddenly ingratiated herself and gained access to Sunday dinners, whose grace and encouragement, whose piety, has made her indispensable to the family, and then, when everyone is asleep, a knife dragged like a zipper from my neck down to my stomach. Blood, death, and rotten sorrow. At the funeral in the tiny rural church, she stands right at the back of the church, smiling.

I'm sorry, Maria. Why have I become so compliant? No outbursts. Only mealtimes, corridors, and treatments. No outside visitors. I've never even visited the city here. I've never set foot in this city.

My voice instead of her creaking one. Views, fresh air. A mixture of tension and all that is meaningless. I am up in a little propeller plane. There's a snowstorm, fog; we're landing. Right before the wheels hit the runway, we lift up again. The plane shakes. Olivia is afraid. I tell her this is nothing out of the ordinary for these pilots. They do it all the time. Up and down, over the mountain. They're the world's best pilots. It's not dangerous. Nothing is dangerous. We were on our way to Västland where your mother lived. I wasn't looking forward to it. We're strapped into this little propeller plane flying from Bergen to Förde. The plane dips again, the roar of the engine. The pilot goes in for the landing at a sharp downward angle. We're landing, I tell Olivia now. The snow, the lights, so much darkness. Soon we'll be on the ground. We're landing.

The force when the engines kick in to rise back up. We rise. The snow out there, us in here. The third time that the plane fails to land I imagine us flying around in circles until the fuel runs out. There is nowhere to land because the earth doesn't exist anymore.

I'm going to recite a poem for you, Maria. This one's for you. You'll recognize it.

Allein

Es führen über die Erde
Straßen und Wege viel,
Aber alle haben
Dasselbe Ziel.

Du kannst reiten und fahren
Zu zwein und zu drein,
Den letzten Schritt mußt du
Gehen allein.

Drum ist kein Wissen
Noch Können so gut,
Als daß man alles Schwere
Alleine tut.

Herman Hesse, Maria said. A beautiful poem. Frightening, if I may say so, but true.

It's probably not frightening—aloneness—if I think about it. It's just the way it is. For everybody. Do you like it? It was our first German assignment in high school, learning Herman Hesse's "Allein" by heart, I said.

And you still remember it?

Yes, of course.

You have a good memory, Maria said and smiled at me.

I've just always had an easy time learning things by heart, I replied.

I'll be back, Maria said. I'm going to hand out the medications now, and you should probably join in on the afternoon coffee break. You've gotten far too thin. If you don't eat, we'll have to give you nutritional drinks. The next time we see each other, I'll be looking forward to hearing your answer to my question.

I ate a few slices of pound cake and immediately felt sick. I couldn't really handle sugar. My dad was diabetic. He'd pee in a test tube then drop a tablet in to measure his blood sugar. Dark blue was very good. Green okay, red meh; if it went orange, towards yellow, that was really bad. I made a habit of checking what color the test tube was each morning. When Dad and I drove up alone to my cousins' in Vännäs, a little village outside of Umeå, Mom told me to give Dad Dextrosol every other hour, a grape sugar that quickly raised your blood sugar level. It went okay. It was a nice trip. Dad was in a good mood and he taught me how to cross-country ski in a trail of electric lights. We went skiing every night. I loved it. Dad's sister Mona seemed irritated when she looked at Dad. I liked my cousins Peter and Petrus very much.

They were so different. Peter was good-humored, fun. Later in life he became a policeman and now he lives with his family in the parental home he's taken over. Petrus is a very good poet. I'm proud of him and mention that we're cousins whenever I get the chance. Petrus is very much his own person. He knows how he wants to live. He has such a nice family, fishing and poems.

Peter and Petrus. Urban and Ulf, my cousins up in Luleå, who were much older than I was and who I had so violently admired when I was small. It made me sad not to have access to Norrland anymore, which is what I'd called Norrbotten since I was small. After my wonderful grandmother died, there was nothing left. Happy Ulf and the perhaps more complicated Urban had their families, their fishing, their work, the hunt. Inga-Britt and Stig had gotten old.

But I digress, Maria. I'm going to answer your question. When you have time, of course.

I have time now, Maria said. But first I'll fix myself a cup of tea.

I'll come with you, I said. I stood by the coffee cart and spent a long time deciding between tea or coffee. Coffee caused my worry to spread and sped up my heart rate, I should really stop drinking coffee, but I took a small cup anyway. I might have been nervous, but I didn't want to acknowledge it. We walked back to my room together and Maria sat on the chair and gave me an encouraging look. I thought, I'm going to get this over with so I can be left in peace, but the moment took hold of me and I became afraid of what I might say. I'll jump right in, I told myself.

I was doing vocational training at a school. I'd been on disability leave for so many years the people who handle that kind of thing got sick of it. Is there nothing you can do?

My friend helped me find a place doing vocational training at the school her daughter attended. I went there every morning. At first it was confusing. I sat next to the fourth-graders and helped them with everything. Language, they'd just started with English. Even math. It made me happy to be able to understand and explain the simplest things, and when the day was over I took the middle-school math books with me, which I'd found in the teacher's lounge, and did sums at home. Everything I hadn't understood as a child. The rage when Dad waited for me to come home from school so he could serve up the speech that he'd been concocting the second he heard me unlock the door.

Pelle has thirteen oranges and gives three to Nora, then they go to the market and buy one and a half kilos of apples, which cost seven kronor per kilo. Each kilo is made up of seven apples. They then give half the fruit to Lisa who in turn gives three pieces to Eva. How many fruits do they have in total and how many fruits does each one have? And how much does Pelle have left of his fifty kronor after asking Nora to buy ice cream with the rest of the money?

Ha ha, none of course, Dad laughed, while my brother quickly calculated how many fruits each one had.

I'm not following, I said, and made a sand-wich. While I was buttering the bread he told me how I was supposed to think, but I didn't listen and he asked if we should play cards, so we did, then we had to play chess and when I couldn't anymore he said we could try using the chess books. Do you want to win or lose? Do you want to be Karpov or Kasparov?

So I was spending my days with the students, in awe over how different each of them was. When one particular girl got tired or bored during the after-school program, she could be very dramatic, and I thought she was probably trying to test me too because she'd screamed about wanting to die. I brought it up with her dad.

Well then, now I know what kind of night we have to look forward to, he said. Mean-while he was sighing because I was yet another classroom assistant—and who was I really? What right did I have to be there? Vocational training. That didn't sound good.

Other students didn't say a word, mainly the boys. They rarely took an interest in schoolwork and many of them had fallen far behind. The girls were quicker and already scheming in a studied way. Who would be included? Who would not? The balance of power in the class could suddenly shift, one false step would do it.

I was happy when a boy, who the teachers had identified as having difficulties with both his schoolwork and his mood, transferred to, well, I can't call it my class, but I will anyway. The teachers in my class were older, experienced, and the boy made quick progress with his schoolwork. Sitting next to him, helping, was fun. He was monosyllabic and would simply up and leave the classroom to go sit outside. I'd follow him, sit next to him and not say anything for a long time. Just sit with him. Sometimes we sat there for a whole class plus the break after. Finally we started talking to each other. He talked about his interests. Drums. He told me about different drummers and bands I hadn't always heard of and I asked about his own drumming, which he'd recently taken up. They never had a problem with him at the Culture School next door, and I'd accompany him there during class time. It started going better for him in school, even if he kept going out into the corridors all of a sudden and for no apparent reason. Because I always followed him out it got to be easy to see if he was in the mood to talk, or if he wanted to sit in silence. We connected somehow and I was so happy the time he turned to me and smiled.

I was only supposed to be at the school for one term, the length of the vocational training, and during my placement there was no talk of me getting hired. Who knows what I would've said if they'd asked. I had no teacher training and didn't want to study to become a teacher either, but I liked being there. Waking up every morning, working a full day, and going home again. Getting to be the boy's assistant and then going home and doing sums in the evening. Understanding what I hadn't bothered with as a child. I never told anyone. About me sitting there doing middle-school math. It was fun. Finally I'd mastered it.

A few years earlier I had debuted with a poetry collection and then worked as a dramaturge at a large theater and so of course it felt like I was selling myself short by doing vocational training at a school. In the intervening years I had fallen ill for the first time, and afterwards was no longer as tough when I was back at my apartment wondering what I was going to do.

The assistant job really suited me. Every day had been if not good then at least okay. I wasn't happy, but I didn't have anxiety. At least I was doing something. The days passed. At graduation when the term was over I stood in the classroom scooping ice cream and singing summer songs with the kids. Rehearsing with them had been fun, but I hadn't thought about their parents being there for the real performance. Me, who wasn't much younger than they were, singing in chorus with their children, like an idiot.

I looked down at the floor and scooped ice cream. I was only biding my time until it was over. I heard the last person leave the classroom and exhaled. I started cleaning away the ice cream dribbles from the desks, wiping away sprinkles, but still I felt ashamed when I was suddenly face to face with the mother of Ville, the boy I'd assisted.

I want to thank you for what you've done for Ville. Truly, thank you. It has meant so much.

We looked at each other and both welled up and the tears were about to fall so I said to the floor: It's nothing.

That's a good memory, I said to Maria and left the room because the tears had come back as I talked about Ville, which Maria had noticed, so she gave me free rein out in the corridor.

Is this really all I remember? The beginning, but not the end. The children, one after another at a pace that meant I was always pregnant again by their first birthday. I remember every film we watched, the mood in the apartment, the porridge, the bodies, the parents' co-op I liked so much. I remember their different personalities. They were so different. Looked so different. What a joy. I never stopped being fascinated by who they were. We talked about the children a lot, laughed and were delighted, the many beds they never slept in. The nights with their bodies so close. When one of them woke up and at first I couldn't tell who had been whimpering in their sleep. I remember the parks, the beaches. They soon learned to speak in long sentences. They learned to swim just as fast. I was happy every day. No, you'd say. You spent one week a month in bed. Yes, but the other weeks I was happy and did everything. Sure, my mother often came down to help out. You didn't like it, but you tolerated it so you could write undisturbed. You wrote and wrote, spent time with the children, wrote and wrote.

I wrote, too. When Josef, our youngest, started in daycare I started writing short stories. I had been offered a space in my friends' lovely house. I'd sit in a room on the top floor where I could look out over the garden. Sometimes they were home during the day and we'd chat and occasionally they'd cook for me.

The first time I sat down at my assigned, beautiful spot, I opened my computer and wrote the first story in one go. I didn't change a word. Right then I understood that all I had to do was write. I had managed to coax the poetry collection out of myself somehow. This was different. I should've never given up that spot in my new friends' house with the garden in town. Who knows why one day I found myself sitting in a shared room in a nearby apartment block. It became harder and harder to go to that new space. My anxiety got worse and worse. That one week a month became more and more difficult.

I remember the time you and I visited the psychiatric clinic. We spoke with a woman, blonde, not that old. I described my situation and she recommended certain medications, but what scared me was that she mentioned electroconvulsive therapy as a good alternative. Both you and I said it wasn't on the cards. Still, she continued to describe electroconvulsive therapy as a good and gentle option. It's not like how it was in the old movies anymore, she said.

One Flew Over the Cuckoo's Nest, I said.

I was mostly thinking about *Gökboet*, she said, which lots of people have seen and have been frightened by.

I didn't tell her that we were talking about the same film.

So what's it like, then? I said. You don't get electricity shot through your head anymore? Well, yes, she admitted, but the electricity is carefully regulated. It's like rebooting a computer.

Rebooting a computer? And if you've forgotten to save something ... what happens then? I asked, mostly to unsettle her, but then she admitted to there being some side effects, including memory loss, but that most memories came back. As we said, it's not on the cards; we got up to leave. What a feeling it was to get up and walk out with you then. A few years later, when I'd been committed to that city's version of a psychiatric ward, a slimy Norwegian doctor spoke to me in your presence about how he'd been mulling over what to say to me. He'd read your books and wanted very much to immerse himself in them further, and his way of speaking irritated us both. He turned to you, as though I were of lesser mind. You got up and told him the meeting was over.

Terrible things happened there. Back then, I still had enough strength to refuse the offer of the ever-so-popular electroconvulsive therapy. I wasn't involuntarily committed, so they couldn't do what they liked with me, like they could later in the city by the water.

The first time I went there, the on-call doctor interviewed me and the two people who'd accompanied me. You were at home with the children. The doctor didn't want to stop talking. I had to interrupt him and point out that my friend and her husband had left their aging father looking after their children and it was probably time for them to get home. He'd finally stopped talking, but he still had hold of their hands as though he never wanted to let go. Once they had left, he turned to me. I'll accompany you to the ward.

In the elevator he offered me a cigarette and said, Enjoy your last minutes of freedom.

That was a cursed ward and when the time came for me to leave it for good, it was like in a movie. You'd risen from your chair, looked the doctor in the eye, and said, Come on, Linda. You'll never have to set foot in here again.

The two of us walked out. No one stopped us as we walked through the corridors. The edges of our vision seemed to be burning as though we'd left everything behind us in flames.

Several years later I read in the newspaper about a young man hanging himself with a belt in that same ward. With a belt? Didn't every intern know to search the incoming patients and confiscate anything they could harm themselves or others with? I'd been searched every time I had arrived. Nail scissors, tweezers, pens, shoelaces. You don't miss a belt. I felt for the boy who had died. I felt compelled to do a radio documentary about the case; I had all of the perspectives, because I myself had been treated there. Not to mention, my education was in radio production and I'd already made two radio documentaries. I knew what it was like to be involuntarily committed and to want to die.

I had planned everything out my first night at the ward in Stockholm, back when I was young and it was my first time in a place like that. The second I set foot in Katarina House, I knew no help was to be found there. This here is hell. I managed to get permission to pick up some clothes the next day with my mother. I knew exactly at which step I'd need to make a run for it on the stairwell—then I'd open my apartment door and dash towards the window, open that, and jump before Mom could catch me. That day my mother and I walked from the hospital to my apartment. I walked quickly and didn't look before crossing the street. Mom insisted on going to Konsum and buying grapes and other treats for me to have at the ward later. I knew I had to be inside my building before I could start running. If I had run from her at Konsum she would've screamed for everybody in the grocery store to stop me. And her scream is so loud, she would've succeeded. I had my key in hand the whole way. I lived on the third floor, and after the first flight of stairs I started to run. Once inside the apartment I was sure I had a big enough head start. There were only a few meters to the window, which I tore open, and I climbed into the frame, ready to jump, I might have hesitated for a second, I must have because Mom caught the hem of my jeans and dragged me to the floor. She must have had superhuman strength. It was a matter of life or death. I got up and we started fighting. I hit her and she hit me. I wrenched myself free and ran into the kitchen, pushed the refrigerator on top of her, and opened the other window, but I hadn't even managed to get into the window frame before she caught up with me. We kept fighting and suddenly we were back in the other room. She wrestled me down and lay on top of me and managed to call the police. I don't remember the minutes before the police arrived. I had given up. Two police officers came into the apartment. One man and one woman. The man went to calm Mom and the woman stood next to where I was sitting on the floor. She looked down at me and said these exact words: You who have your own apartment and everything, so many people your age don't have anywhere to live. Think about that!

I remember her pulling me up from the floor and pushing me onward down the stairs. My mother followed behind with the other officer. I don't remember her crying. We drove back to the hospital in the police car and once we'd arrived my mother said,

Now it's your turn to take care of her. Can you see now how sick she is?

I don't know what I did, but I remember being given a shot and Mom asking for a painkiller for her headache before she left.

She knew she wasn't allowed to hug me or anything. I remember her saying, It's going to be fine, Linda. Stay here. It's going to be fine.

It wasn't fine, but after a few years I stopped drifting in and out of the ward and slowly got better. I spent a lot of time at Mom's place in the country, reading children's books in bed. Mom was so afraid of the train tracks along the bottom of the property, before the lake and the swimming dock. For no reason. The train was never an option for me. I had failed to take my own life. Sixteen years would pass before I tried again.

I moved back in to my apartment and soon thereafter started doing the vocational training at the school.

I couldn't go back to that horror-ward in Malmö to interview the staff on duty when the boy was admitted and during his brief stay. I had already done a radio documentary about my years at Katarina House as my final project at the University College of Film, Radio, Television and Theatre. That would have to be enough, I thought. I didn't have it in me to immerse myself in the boy's case, even if I hated that hospital more than anything else.

This much I knew: People with a death wish have a plan. Maybe the boy had lied and said he only needed to be there for a few days. Maybe he had been admitted of his own free will. I didn't know the details, but I know that people with plans usually carry them out unless they are stopped. A belt. Damn. I had other things to think about. To my relief, *Mission: Investigate* ended up doing a story on the case.

We rented a house in Österlen for a week one summer. I know we did, but I remember none of that week. I'm sure we swam at the white sand beach by Knäbäckshusen and drove around the rapeseed fields, slender red poppies lining the road. I'm sure we talked about the beauty of it all. I'm sure we were happy. I'm sure you were even more taken by the landscape than I was.

I remember us looking at a house for sale. Three buildings in an L-shape. I remember the beautiful, manicured garden. I've never lived in the countryside. It was all new to me. I don't have a driver's license. But oh, I was taken. The mood in the garden was calm and composed. The steps on the side of the house that I immediately took to be mine were a good spot. Sitting on steps has always spoken to me. Reading, looking out over the garden, which under our care grew wilder and wilder. I never touched the garden, that was all you. I was naive and probably thought the garden would always look as nice as the day we bought the house. I didn't realize it was a full-time job.

The first time I cut the grass you said you'd never seen anything so disorganized.

Here you go, the lawn is yours.

You dove into gardening. I did nothing, which must've irked you no end. Me not trying at all. Surely busying myself in the garden would've had a calming effect, but I wasn't interested, was afraid, snipped a little here and there, plucked some plums and blackcurrants and ignored the rest.

The couple who'd lived in the house before us had kept everything in order. The woman, our neighbors told us, was always gardening. It had been paradise then.

I wouldn't be so sure, I thought, because the woman had left little notes written in ink all around the house.

Under a window frame, up on a bedroom wall.

Days that resemble each other are the best days, she had written, and, *I don't see you anymore, you are someone else, but I am the same.*

We talked about erasing her messages, but both agreed that her writing should be preserved.

We were at your mother's house in Västland when you made an offer on the house and it was accepted and we were so happy and we celebrated. Further down the street was a small school, which the children would attend. A school that would shut down within two years. So it was the school bus to Löderup instead. After a while this didn't feel like a good fit, so they switched to a cute, very good, clean, friendly, and beautiful Montessori school at the regiment in Ystad. You drove the children back and forth. For a few years there, things seemed promising.

*

A decision must survive two frames of mind. This is an old legal maxim and is perhaps the saying that has helped me out most in my life. As long as I waited for the time of the month to come when nothing seemed bright, far more than half of my brilliant ideas would disappear. I tried to get to know the remaining few first. Still, you can't be cowardly. The ability to carry out an action decisively is a talent in itself.

I was out of step. My convictions didn't last very long. The worry spread and my inability to sense what was good for me or what was bad for me made things difficult. I've always admired those friends I have who know what they prefer to do in a situation. I never learned how. I'm like a beginner at life in every moment. I like being out with the children and going to movies. This I know. I had become an asocial with a great need for human contact. Researchers are now talking about how loneliness is genetic.

I like sayings and old words of wisdom. They have survived through time and I collected them and jotted them down in a special notebook. Speech is silver, silence is golden. I collected old farmers' proverbs. Think twice, act once, seek counsel from those who know you before following your impulses. Take care of your friends, but only spend time with people who wish you well. Don't make enemies, be kind. Always be kind, you have no idea what other people have been through. Everybody carries something inside them that they themselves don't understand, so always be kind. Kind and thoughtful, but run away from people who drain your energy. Always be considerate towards your children. Be patient with your children. Love them every second, but don't let them drift alone into a world only they understand. Take an interest in your children, encourage their interests without killing their curiosity with your own enthusiasm, like I did with Anna and karate. We stood in a square around the room, all of us parents who'd brought their children to try out karate for the first time. The sensei started by saying that karate begins and ends with respect; the second thing he said was that no onlookers were allowed. Everyone participates. Surprised, we parents took off our shoes. It was a fun class. Simple exercises that made a big difference. Beauty in the movements, the body in balance. I got really into it and unfortunately made that far too clear.

You're the one who wants to take karate, Anna said afterwards when I was talking about the class. I immediately realized my mistake.

Out in the country everything had sort of fallen silent for me, even if things with me were getting better. I wrote a lot, but you and I spoke less and less. Still, I'd asked you if we shouldn't have another baby. No, you said, absolutely not. Three children is enough. But you got used to the idea, perhaps without realizing it, and when we flew to Australia for one of your assignments we were suddenly full of optimism. On the flight home, I was pregnant with Sara.

What happened in the months before she was born can't be explained. Maybe I want to defend myself. The first three pregnancies had all gone so well. I didn't take any pills, was hale, hardy. I was a mother. I'd never known such strength. Unbroken motivation and love.

I fell sick during my pregnancy with Sara. I lounged around in the hot bedroom with only this unbearable life as company. Anxiety was everywhere. It got harder and harder to breathe. I sank so deep into myself that I lost all perspective. Realizing it was over. This is what I remember. I couldn't manage without the pills this time. Maybe my body had gotten used to them. Or was it something else, something I absolutely could not get my head around?

I know what happened next, Maria said. I was with you the whole time you were here. You don't need to keep going.

I couldn't speak. I couldn't do anything. After several weeks without any sign of life other than violent anxiety and a strong sense that I couldn't handle this, I gave up.

I don't know why the depression became an abyss at that exact moment.

Why did I take every pill I had and hide them in a glass in the morning? In the evening I took them all then went into the bedroom where you were reading and lay down next to you. You turned off the light and said good night and I said good night to you against my will. I knew how important not talking to you was. If I said anything to you, I wouldn't be able to pull this off. I hated having said good night to you. I knew it would be the last thing I'd say to you. I counted silently to drown everything else out.

How could I do that, Maria? I was pregnant. The children were sleeping in the next room.

You were very sick, Maria said. You should've come here much sooner.

We'd gone to see a doctor the week before. He'd confirmed that I was in a deep depression and had asked if I wanted to kill myself. I said no. But the truth was, death and dying were all I thought of.

You'd called our friends Mia and Henrik, who came to take care of the children. They arrived in a flash, aware of how serious the situation was. They were both adrenaline junkies. They offered paragliding for tourists and had a flight school. Henrik was the one at the wheel of the Jeep. Mia told me this after. She added that the children had been at their place when the ambulance sped by, sirens off. I don't dare imagine what they might have been thinking, feeling.

Mia said the paramedics revived me immediately and that you'd said I'd sternly instructed them to take it easy. Mia said your voice had been full of warmth and love as you'd said this.

She said the children had had a lovely summer. You drove to the beach every day. Made sure they'd have it good and things would be as normal as possible. I wish I'd been there that summer. That I'd never done anything unforgivable. I wish I was someone else.

When she was born, I went on, she was as whole and herself and beautiful and delightful as the others had been and I prayed to

God that I'd be able to take care of her, and I was.

We were so grateful that she was healthy; I had taken a lot of pills.

I know, said Maria. But nothing that would transfer to the child. I know what you took that time. I was there too, planning your continued dosage with the supervising physician. Do you remember her? A woman, a former gynecologist and midwife. Very experienced. I promise you this, you weren't given anything that could've harmed the child.

That was never my fear, Maria. I was sure she was in perfect health the whole time. I knew she was even before I held her in my arms. I just knew.

She's so funny, Maria. So lovely and alive. With so many older siblings, she's learned everything faster than the others. She always has a glimmer in her eye. She's a joy to be with. She finds clever ways to help out. It never ceases to surprise me.

I knew that what I'd done had raised a wall in you. You will never stop blaming me for this.

Never forgive me. I understand. However, there's one thing I don't understand. How could you let me spend weeks on end in bed? Why didn't you dump me at the hospital like you had done the other times? You knew me, after all. What did you think I was thinking about? Did you think I was spending all that time in bed lazing around? Questions that were never asked.

Sara's first year was lovely, as all the first years had been with the other children. We were as amazed as ever by the little one and she was the focus of everyone's attention. You took care of her at night so I could sleep. Suddenly we were hearing how important sleep was. I didn't like it. I'd nursed the other children at night and had never slept better.

We did so much with the children. Outings to the beach where the wind took hold of the girls' long hair. Josef running across the sand. It resembled joy. Was joy. Time passed and we were so consumed that I almost never reflected on how we stopped being close after that time in Australia. I understood the implication, but I still tried to explain it away by thinking it was no surprise. Sara was little, I thought, but not that little. It would pass. Deep down I knew this wasn't true.

I'm sorry, but I have to go, Maria said. I think you should get out of this room. I'm going to ask Aalif to stay with you for a while. I don't want you to be alone. You two can go for a walk in the corridor.

Maria left to hand out pills. I barely noticed. The heat in this little room that was never aired out made me feel sick; or was it what I'd just told her that made me feel like I couldn't breathe? I wasn't getting any air. Like hell was I going to do square breathing. I grabbed the notebook which I kept on the small table and wrote these words.

I'd gone to the summer house to write. But I wasn't in a writing zone, I was outside of one, where the words would not come. I stared into the computer. Typed a few sentences that made me hate myself. Directionless language. No scent to follow. No vision. Nothing. Just vile words. As dumb as the diaries I was always starting as a child. Ten pages of repetitions, claustrophobia, and also a childish self-righteousness. Then nothing. I had begun over one hundred diaries as a child. Written a few pages, left the rest empty. I could never see anything through. I couldn't write. That's how it was. I couldn't, I couldn't, until at some point I could and then I wrote blindly. I was sleepwalking. No, the opposite: I was wide awake. I couldn't stop writing.

I've never actually written anything significant alone. When I've written, really written, it has been as an overgrown child. Fully cared for and fed. I heard the children in the background, their noise became a kind of calming, ambient music. I wasn't alone with myself in the dark. My mother was often with me when I was deep in my writing. She took care of the children. Of everything. I was alone and yet not. You were as often away as at home when I was writing.

Sometimes my ambition was to write as much as possible so you'd be impressed when you came home and would read what I had done.

I was irritated with myself. Circled through the usual mocking thoughts. I remember that instead of trying to sit back down at the computer I got into bed and fell right asleep. A knock on the door woke me up several hours later. I woke up sweaty and angry at myself. The sun through the window was baking. I was sticky and bloated from having overslept. I couldn't actually handle the summer. The sharp light. The unbearable heat. The children's summer vacations not being as rich and full of escapades as I would've liked. What kind of memories would they have? What kind of magic? Or would they create that magic on their own later? What could I know about their future childhood memories? They still preferred the outdoor pool one bus stop away to the ocean. I was the only one fantasizing about long outings and beautiful landscapes. The summer was one long hunt for shade. I had sunburn as early as April. Sandy, wet towels. I wasn't especially fond of looking out over the sea. Its total openness frightened me. The ocean wasn't like the lakes I swam in growing up. Sörmland's lakes, Trolltjärn outside Bergnäs at Grandma's. The water at Ingarö. I wasn't used to the ocean and only learned to appreciate it years later.

I was furious when I opened the door and what looked like a retired couple, or whatever they were, said they were here on an errand. They had come to visit you. With irritation I pointed at your house and they thanked me kindly and finally walked away. I imagined the scene, the freshly showered seniors walking into the building where you were working. It was impossible to breathe in there. The house was full of books, prizes, and cigarettes. Cigarettes everywhere. There were maybe fifty cups full of cigarette butts and the whole house stank of smoke. I never understood how you could sit there breathing that air all day long and I constantly worried you'd die of a heart attack and I'd be left to take care of the children all on my own. There was no doubt in my mind I wouldn't be able to handle it.

We were constantly fighting about cigarettes and your chain-smoking. I preached about your responsibility towards the children, but a doctor had examined your lungs;

they were like a youngster's, he'd said. You had even taken a DNA test, you really were interested in yourself, and the results suggested that a long and healthy life awaited you. What about heart attacks? I countered. Your mother had a heart attack, after all. She also smoked incessantly. My own mother had had a heart attack, as had her father, my grandfather, who died at our country house. The ambulance that never arrived. This sudden death on our patio.

In my family all the women who smoked also had chronic obstructive pulmonary disease, so, of all people, I definitely should not start smoking. I was scared to death of my own genes and inclinations and I'd often thought you were the perfect father for our children. Your vigorous disposition would get passed down to them. Only you could wipe out my inherent weaknesses. Madness, COPD, and alcoholism.

Me, I only drank a little now, maybe four times a year, on special occasions. In my youth, I'd already been drunk enough for a lifetime. You didn't drink either and I never let on what a shame I thought it was, because you were delightful when you drank. So open, with none of your usual restraint, like when we first fell in love.

We were drunk on love and alcohol our whole first summer together, but had sobered up as fall neared. I described the feeling of landing in a reality that no longer adapted to us in a short story I wrote years later, when we already had three children and had moved to a city I could never wrap my head around. A freer place, but one I never got to know.

We closed ourselves off like you close up a summerhouse. Efficiently, heads held high and with one last glance to make sure nothing was left behind.

I started feeling cold again. Paying bills. You started writing and this made you even happier than falling in love. You had a hard time writing after your first book and this reunion with yourself was a joy and a power that exceeded all else. I knew this then, and later in life I would experience the same happiness once I started writing again.

I started at the radio program at the University College of Film, Radio, Television and Theatre and became pregnant. Everything was incredibly exciting. We were both doing our very best. It was a memorable time. A fantastic time. Always in action. No dips and no months of shapelessness and restless tedium as usually follow falling in love. Well, not only after falling in love. I had as easy a time creating, having a good spell, as I did entering a downward spiral.

Later, there was a kind of rage over it being over, and us becoming normal to each other again; meanwhile I was so busy with school and the pregnancy, which filled me up completely. This wonder, this almost tortuous joy and awe over what was happening inside my body and soul. I was incredibly grand and consumed with myself and the growing child. Not to speak of after she was born. We couldn't stop looking at her. All I wanted to do was look at this child. Our Anna who was the most fantastic person the world had ever seen. She was so safe in my arms, and the fact that I could generate comfort was revolutionary.

Once the retired couple had left I fell back asleep. When I woke up I was incredibly disappointed with myself for letting the day slip away and, instead of trying to write in its last hour, I went to you. Yes, why? Well, to complain, apparently. I was bad at shaping my life, and my loneliness was difficult to handle, at least that's what I was telling myself as I walked into your house and sat down on the orange sofa.

What did the seniors want? I asked.

You said you didn't want to be interrupted, and instead of dealing with my frustration myself, being aware that I was mad at myself for sleeping the day away, I lashed out at you. I brought up the usual stuff. I hated living in the country. We had to move to Stockholm. You said what you usually said: It won't be better in Stockholm and I've written two books here in a short span of time, haven't I? That means something. You wouldn't have had as easy a time writing in Stockholm. For Christ's sake, I'm an adult now. I would have. I don't think so, you said. On the contrary, being here does you good. You know it does. I knew this to be partly true. I'd had the same thought myself many times, a fear of not being able to write in any other place. As soon as I had the chance, I'd distract myself. I continued my lament—my friends, how I wasn't at all a country person, how I didn't have a driver's license because I was afraid of cars and because a year without incident had to pass before someone like me could be granted a learner's permit. I was afraid of the garden and of you hating me. I wrapped up my harangue with: We should get a divorce. I often said things I absolutely didn't mean in order to start a fight. To pour out all my unsorted feelings. To be able to cry. Having cried always made me feel better. Everything was actually fine. A cry was all I wanted. Nothing more.

You looked at me for a long time, then you said, Yes, I suppose we should.

You said you'd been considering it for a while.

I want a divorce, you said, and looked me in the eye. I want a divorce.

As always when my existence is threatened, I felt wide awake. I have a sort of readiness for catastrophe; I functioned in ways I never normally could. You used to say I was at my best when it counted and maybe that's why you dared to say what you said. No, you said it because it was true. You'd had enough.

A temporary calm set in, although my heart was beating as though I were facing death. I was facing death. The rest of my life flew past my eyes like a film on fast-forward.

Then the moment passed. I was rumbling inside as if I were near a motorway. Everything was moving too quickly and I was so sensitive to noise that I wanted to flee this din. I won't be able to handle it. I can handle anything, but not this.

I fell from one moment into the next, each more horrific than the previous. I saw the children all in a row, much smaller than they actually were. Thin arms, unblinking eyes. Then these words tumbling through me: This, too, I must bear.

I knew when you were serious about something, it was set in stone. Bells rang in my ears. Yes, this is exactly how it went. I heard bells ringing.

Then there was that drive, the first blossoming before summer took off.

In the midst of fear, this experience of joy because we were talking to each other. A conversation being conducted without lies.

The lies came later. Not lies exactly, but a radical difference in how the story of this divorce would be presented to the children.

You'd decided we wouldn't breathe a word about it being you who'd wanted the divorce. There would be no victim, no perpetrator.

We had grown apart, we'd say. After all, it may have been true, but I hadn't been aware of that when we gathered the children around the table to tell them that from now on we'd be living apart. The children told us later that they'd thought they would be getting a new sibling. They each took the news differently. One feared change, another was more adventurous and immediately pictured the modern town house that we'd secretly bought for me.

I imagined dragging myself through existence, but trying to do my best. Cast out into a strange place where I'd be around nothing of importance to me. I would live in a vacuum. And I didn't want to do that to the children, so I demanded we move to my hometown in order to fortify the structure of my life. The children would be with me in a city I knew inside and out. Their lives would be filled with people who were important to me. To them. And when I didn't have the children I could go to the cinema, the theater, meet friends I sorely missed, though I could never persuade myself to call them.

But I quickly gave up. The children shouldn't have to experience another rupture after the shock of the divorce. That much I had to understand. Yes, perhaps it was true. Of course it was true. One day when I took the bus into the little senior citizens' city, Hell, I went to the swimming hall. I've always loved swimming and right there in the pool from one moment to the next I decided I would be able to live in this city after all, because I could swim. The swimming hall was right by my new home, which so far I'd barely set foot in. Then there was your curse, you hadn't intended it to be one, but that's what it became, what you so often returned to, and what I feared deep down was true: You can't write in that city.

Couldn't I write in that city? I didn't know. But why not? Of course I could.

The children would only have to move fifteen minutes away from the village we'd lived in together. I don't know whether or not I regret it. Yes, I do. I regret it.

I would show them every inch of where I was from. Ride the subway with them all across the city. I would become a happier person. A better mother. I would become myself. Not an incapacitated mother without a driver's license in some lousy hellscape. Or would I? I wasn't sufficiently convinced. No. I comforted myself with the fact that I'd be able to visit the city when the children weren't with me. But where would I stay? Not with Mom, sometimes with friends, but they wouldn't have enough space for me. Well, my best friend would, but she had a family. I couldn't impose on them so much.

Goddammit, aren't I an author? My publisher can pay for my hotel.

But I knew I could never ask them to. Unless it was in a specific context involving them, and those were few and far between.

That nightmare trip we took to Crete. It was your idea. We'd announce our divorce and some days later we'd all go to Greece. I understood your line of thinking. We would show the children that we were friends and that they weren't in any danger. I was also glad to be given some sort of respite. Even though it was staged, it felt right. I had loved Greece since childhood, when I'd taken trips to Hydra with my friend's family. An island free from cars. There was one fire engine and one garbage truck, the rest of the traffic was handled by donkeys, which appeared in every alley. The first time I visited I was six years old. I had spent a month on Hydra with my best friend Michaela and her mother and father. I can't remember ever being afraid or homesick. Michaela and I ran down to the bakery every morning and bought bread and baked goods dusted white with powdered sugar, which we christened "moon cakes." I taught my friend to swim, and to celebrate we were each allowed an ice cream of our choosing. We both picked one with Charlie Chaplin drawn in vanilla and chocolate.

As a child I was afraid of Charlie Chaplin.

His black eyes and his walk creeped me out. Now I love Charlie Chaplin and prize him above all other artists. During the silent film module of my film studies course, we watched all of Chaplin's films on a big screen and it was a delight. I especially loved the cuff dance in *Modern Times,* in which his cheat sheet of song lyrics drops from his cuff the second he glides on stage. Those first steps, when he's trying to look for the piece of paper without the audience noticing, are wonderful.

Just as wonderful is the scene where he unknowingly becomes the leader of a demonstration and is arrested. By the time he has served his sentence, he doesn't want to leave his prison.

Suddenly I was fantasizing about life in another country. Far away from here. Across the sea.

I pictured myself with a key in my hand. I'd bought a small apartment without viewing it first. Here is where I will live out my days, I thought as I unlocked the green door.

It was a two-room apartment with a small

kitchen. The children weren't there. Maybe they hadn't been born yet. I was alone with my suitcase in this furnished apartment. Old chairs around a small kitchen table, a gas stove, a lace curtain hanging in the window facing the backyard.

The living room was the kind of peaceful room I've always dreamed of, and could never achieve myself. I have no talent for homemaking. Here, I didn't have to try.

I was not responsible for this apartment and yet it was instantly mine.

A small desk by the window. There I would sit and write until my life one day was over. I didn't long for a life like this there, because there it was unquestionably possible. I didn't need anyone and no one needed me.

The apartment had been a gift from God.

He hadn't asked anything of me in return. Still, I would pray to him five times a day. Pray for forgiveness. Forgive me for not wanting to live.

I wish I could give you LSD. LSD has a remarkable effect on ennui. Too bad your country hasn't come this far yet.

My name is Attilla. I'm the new chief physician. What an abysmal system you have here. This country is so rigid.

Yes, truly, I agreed.

Did you like the apartment?

You know about it?

We held a séance, you and I. Let's say I have access to your dreams and fantasies. I was about to recommend an immediate move to another country.

I'm afraid that won't work. I'm a mother of four.

You're not much of a mother to them.

You're wrong.

No need to worry about your children. They can live with you, but you can't stay in this country.

Who are you?

I'm the new chief physician.

I recognize you.

We old souls recognize each other. He winked.

Are you here to pick me up?

Do you want to be picked up by a strange man? He smiled.

No, but I thought—

What did you think?

That you were here to pick me up.

Take a seat here with me, he said. I sat in his lap.

I like you, I said.

Why am I here? Just tell me.

I don't know. What do you think?

Attilla. I liked the sound of it. A lot. He would free me from my torments. It would take something major for me to resist my weaknesses. My strength.

Don't forget why you're here, I ventured.

I know why I'm here. To turn this building upside down.

I'm your partner in crime. Give me a sign.

I'll issue your release papers in a week's time, which leaves us seven days and nights.

What are we going to do?

Erotics are an equal substitute for this electricity they're fiddling with, which might be good for you to know.

True, I had become something of a nun. You're joking, I said.

Not necessarily, but of course I'm not going to break any rules. That would be totally out of character.

He vanished before my eyes.

I was on Hydra again. I was twelve years old and it was Easter.

Springtime on the island felt completely different to summer. The rhythm was different in summer, with the bathing ships going out to the swimming spots after breakfast, and us keeping an eye out for the waves in the wake of the large boats. *Midnight Express*, *Apollo*, *Flying Dolphin*.

I really liked being on Hydra, where my best friend's dad had a charming small house at the top of a lane.

So it was Easter and we were going to go to the square along with everyone else on the island.

The little square was crowded. I was afraid of losing sight of Michaela. In the middle of the square hung a dressed-up straw doll on a hanger. Michaela's dad said it was Judas.

A hush descended when the young men of the village stepped forward. They were all dressed identically—black pants, white shirt, suspenders, a black hat, and a rifle. The priest gave the signal and stepped aside and the men shot Judas. I was scared and stunned. I'd never experienced anything like this. The gun smoke, the tributes. The square emptying and the party breaking out, the procession down to the harbor where the boats were waiting; they were set alight and pushed out to sea. The burning boats were visible all night, drifting into the distance.

The next day I asked Michaela's grandmother to tell me about Jesus.

We were alone for several hours and her story frightened me. I didn't dare interrupt her. I was hungry and needed the bathroom, yet I sat there transfixed.

Afterward Michaela said, as if she believed she had the upper hand:

I heard you wanted to know all about Jesus.

It was humiliating. This sudden reversal of status.

Forever shaking hands. Presenting yourself. Meeting. The meeting was important. To look each other in the eyes.

I didn't want to look anyone in the eye and this was observed, noted, and explained. I listened to the explanation. The takeaway was that I had to look the person I was speaking to in the eye. I understood. I look everyone in the eye now. Sometimes the person you're looking at is there. Sometimes not.

Do you feel better?

I feel better.

Can you take this test?

Yes, I can.

The self-evaluation test. Every answer is given in degrees. With gradients ranging from bearable to unbearable. I circle the answer I think fits best. It's not as easy as you think. Several questions give me pause, then I circle the number that fits well enough.

I hand the paper to the doctor, who tallies up the score. A clear improvement, he says.

Yes, I say.

Do you want to start with conditional leave?

Yes.

Shall we say for an hour tomorrow?

Yes.

What are you thinking of doing?

I'm going to buy a guitar.

That'll cost you. A long discussion ensued about whether or not I was allowed to buy a guitar. Was it impulsive? Reckless? Secretly manic?

Do you play guitar?

No.

So why do you want to buy a guitar?

Because there's no piano here. I'll teach myself. Just a few chords. I'm thinking about buying a book for beginners. I'm going to teach myself a song.

Which song?

That's my business.

I'm just curious.

Are you still writing?

Yes.

You're not really eating. Do you know why?

My thyroid is out of whack because of the medications, and the food is hard to swallow.

Your thyroid, yes. We'll look into it. Is an emergency test okay?

You have permission to buy a guitar. Do you know where the music store is?

Yes.

The meeting is over. All rise and look each other in the eye as they shake hands.

*

On Crete, our final trip, everything was dead and uncomfortable. No one was happy. The pool you'd imagined the children swimming in was ice cold. Our brief conversations were, on your side, full of boredom; on my side, full of paralysis, the children, the children, the wonderful children, and fear.

The trips in the rental car to beaches that were much too far away. The silence, the questions, and the children's striking ability to nonetheless play.

Our eldest couldn't express herself through play anymore; she was entering puberty. A vulnerable age. Different vulnerabilities at different ages. Everyone was happy in their own way and everyone was uncertain. But not Sara, not yet, she was too small. Just over a year.

Most of all I liked lying on the made bed in the cross-breeze in the afternoon, reading with Sara sleeping beside me and marveling at the lizards as they ran across the wall.

It's mealtime, Aalif said. I didn't respond. He asked if he should bring me a tray of food and I said yes please, and kept writing.

I remember the first time I realized you didn't want to be with me anymore.

It was at an airport. All these airports. All these trips back and forth across the globe.

Kastrup was in chaos. We were there two hours before departure. The lines weren't moving. There were so many people who weren't getting anywhere and just as many guards. What happened? I asked one of them. They didn't respond. Is it some fucking terror attack or what?

You flashed me an angry look.

I'm joking, I said.

I was pretty worked up because I couldn't handle lines and I was afraid of flying and irritated at you for not starting the day with enthusiasm. Such as: Off we go, what fun it will be to see the apartment in Venice again, that lovely apartment my publisher is renting. It will be our third visit. This time we're really going to get out and explore Venice and swim at the Lido on the hottest days.

We'd carried children and strollers up and down every flight of stairs in Venice many times, but this time would be the last. I didn't know that then, there in line, though maybe I had a misgiving, or a taste in my mouth. In any case the vibe was off and it would only get worse and I had shut my eyes to it as one does to the truths one isn't ready to hear. I really wasn't prepared for your resistance when finally it was our turn with the woman at the desk.

They're closing the gate now, she said. It's too late.

Too late?

That's when I let everything brewing inside me come spilling out. You're going to open the gate for us, I screamed. We were here two hours before our flight, like we were supposed to be. This panic is not our fault, it's your fault. Now open the gate.

I have this ability to see black and stop giving a shit. I continued screaming at her. Here are the tickets. You're welcome. Now let us through.

She let us through. I turned to you as we all made our way to the security check and said, Good.

I expected a smile, a token of appreciation.

Her hand was on the alarm, you said. Yeah? You shouldn't scream in front of the children. Yes, but now we're in, which is good, right? No, you said. No? Okay, well, with your method we would've been halfway home on the Öresund Bridge by now. Yes, we would, you said. And that's when I saw it in your face. You didn't want to go to Venice. You were taking the trip out of a sense of duty and you would've rather stayed home, writing. You didn't want to travel. You'd seen her refusal as an opportunity.

We flew to Venice. I don't remember our stay at all. I suppose we went around bemoaning our freedom. Who we had become. Nobody we wanted to know. Maybe this was when you started to think you could simply disembark. Maybe you were already enjoying the free life there in the crowd on the Bridge of Sighs.

In our first year as a couple we visited Venice, both of us for the first time.

I once lived with a friend in Florence for six months right after high school, but we'd never made our way to Venice. We'd driven around Tuscany in her boyfriend's car. We'd read up on all the cities, churches, ruins, and museums, but ultimately I was just along for the ride. I didn't understand what my friend and Stefano, her boyfriend, were talking about, but I didn't mind. Unfortunately all I'd learned of the language were phrases from an Italian novel, which I'd read with a phrasebook alongside:

Tra il dire e il fare c'è di mezzo il mare.

The expression was as if written for me. I never did anything properly. I tired quickly of this beautiful, but meaningless, existence. I was homesick without knowing for what.

I didn't meet anybody I wanted to sleep with, which was a drag; I was nineteen and in Italy, after all. I kissed one person. Michele. He was handsome, but stiff. His kisses were so wet, it felt less like a kiss and more like he was forcing me to swallow his spit. Not to mention that my friend told me off as though she'd had dibs on Michele. This was before she coupled up with Michele's friend Stefano, and I backed down. I didn't want him anyway.

During one of our language lessons at the school, our Italian teacher had said the best way to learn Italian was to get an Italian boyfriend—so it was even sanctioned from above. For a long time, waking up next to someone I didn't want to be with would give me a deep, lingering anxiety. To avoid such embarrassing situations, I wore the ugliest underwear I could get my hands on: Mom's old stage underwear from some play. All the things I came up with to ward off advances. Or to avoid sleeping with someone I was interested in on the very first night. Like a chastity belt. I was convinced that I wouldn't even consider presenting myself in those panties. It almost worked.

I tried to embellish my depression and call it melancholia. There may have been some truth to it, but the actual truth was that I was pretending to play a part in an old Italian film. I was performing my youth. Depressively melancholic, I drifted in the rain through a river of tourists to Santa Maria Croce and had ice cream. It rained the entire fall and the small apartment we lived in on Via del Pellegrino was subterranean, with a few stone steps leading up to the garden. Every morning we wiped up the water that had seeped from the garden onto our kitchen floor.

All the beautiful places. Boredom and melancholy increasingly becoming a real depression. I slept more and more and only got up at night to tag along to Casalinga for a bite before the partying started.

The flood that had submerged large parts of the city in 1966 began to interest me more and more. The downpour that made the River Arno rise six meters in one hour. The entire city was flooded, sixty-six people died and artistic treasures were destroyed.

Arno was as high as during the flood, but since then they'd built drainage canals, which diverted the rainwater. As for school, the Università per Stranieri, I quit after a few weeks. I roamed the city and felt worse and worse, as happens when I'm not doing anything sensible. I despaired over how I was wasting my youth. You must try your best every day. The anxiety when I slept a day away, several days, made me sweat in the sheets, which were already damp and covered in almond biscotti crumbs.

Before I went to Italy, I'd applied to university so I could keep studying Italian after Christmas. I absolutely did not want to anymore. I didn't understand anything. I would have preferred to have taken a class a level below my friend. I can't learn Romance languages. I'd already tanked French in junior high, so I started taking Italian instead in high school. At the same time I'd also started German, which made sense, was easy to learn, and while I hovered at an average grade in Italian, this was not the case for German, which was my highest grade by a long shot during those three years. My German teacher, Barbara, asked me to help a hopeless student in the afternoons in the run-up to an important test, and I promised I would. A promise that, of course, I did not keep.

I was so done trying to learn Italian that I didn't stop calling the University of Stockholm until I was granted permission to switch from the Italian fiasco to a foundation course in literature.

I counted the days until I could go home.

The Arno rose and rose in the rain. At least it was the right city to be depressed in.

I flew home relieved, moved in with Mom, and started the literature course. My depression magically disappeared. I studied hard to compensate for having wasted half a year. My good, slightly superior mood returned.

Italian and depression? How did I end up here? There wasn't much of that during our first trip to Venice. My suitcase had been lost, it hadn't turned up on the baggage carousel and I had been asked to write my telephone number and our temporary address down and give it to a carabiniere in an information kiosk. The suitcase showed up by courier the day before our departure and I remember us laughing about it. But what did I wear that week? We didn't have a lot of money, so I wouldn't have bought anything new. Did I borrow one of your shirts and go around in the trousers I'd worn on the plane? It was an intimate trip with inspired declarations of love. Everything was meaningful and desired. A dream. No fights, just one sweet moment after the next. The future was unspoken and the present was in every heartbeat. The art, the paintings, which we both considered to be the highest art form. Imagine being able to paint. I remember saying that if I could live my life over again I would learn to play the piano properly. It's not too late, you said. No. It wasn't too late. I decided to contact a piano teacher as soon as we got home and you promised to start painting, which you would end up doing around the time of our divorce. I forgot about the piano once I started at the radio school and soon thereafter became pregnant.

It was also in Venice that I, for the first time, truly understood what you meant with your recurring speech about shame. I'd heard you deliver it on several occasions and related, but I had yet to experience shame with you, unless you count our devastating first encounter. We had read through the beautiful guestbook in the apartment and laughed at certain authors' self-aggrandizing, but still quite wonderful, words:

Today on the loveliest Lido I have, to the delight of myself and others, submerged my body in the Adriatic Sea. Cool at last, I gave no thought to leaving the water. Unbidden, my brother came to mind, whose corpse I never viewed because at the time of his sudden death I found myself in the arms of an exceptionally generous and intelligent hotel hostess and could not be reached. Guilt still sheathes my body and darkens my dreams, rendering it impossible for me to fall back asleep. I opened my eyes and was blinded by the sun. And yet I noticed a pigeon staring at me from the beach and with its loud cooing ... perhaps not quite cooing exactly, oh every devil knows what a pigeon sounds like. When I looked into the eyes of that messenger in disguise I immediately thought of my delicate but starved stomach, and from within this extended moment I received from the pigeon's mouth a directive. Go home to your brother, who awaits you at the post office in Tromsö. This pigeon continued to stare at me in the water, and I do mean stare, and it was this pigeon who in this way ruined my holiday. How could I sit and write in that beautiful apartment when my brother was calling me? Impossible. At the same time I felt honored to be visited upon by revelation as I was, embraced by water and in tears. Sonja is now packing in a hurry so we can make the flight home. I am not leaving the prerequisite bottle of wine behind. Dammit, I won't *even make the flight. I'll have to take the next one. Well, then my wife can go and buy the bottle of wine that is supposed to greet you, you unknown person who will spend time in this magnificent apartment after me. I have now been informed that we will indeed be making the flight. To the airport! Thank you and my apologies. It's just as well. I can't write in foreign countries anyway. I get sick to the stomach. The truth is, I'm helpless. I can't take a step without my poor Sonja by my side, and she's had a pain in her leg for so long. The time is now, goddammit. Thank you and goodbye.*

As the end of our trip neared, the time came for you to write in the guestbook. You wrote a long entry, which was lovely, and then we left Venice.

The guestbook entry tormented you for weeks. You wanted to go back and tear out the pages. It was a lovely piece and I said so, but it didn't help. You bathed in shame for weeks.

Authors should collect what fascinates them. As a child I reread Greek mythology after seeing a children's holiday series on television in which one Greek myth was retold each night leading up to Christmas, like an advent calendar. My mom must have noticed how much I loved this series because she gave me a book on Greek mythology as a Christmas present. I loved that book too. I wish I still had it. The monstrous Medusa on the orange cover with her hair of snakes had frightened me into the deepest obsession. Perseus was standing in front of her using his shield as a mirror so as to avoid looking directly into Medusa's eyes, and that's how he was able to cut off her head.

Wiles, fate, calling.

I was particularly in love with the story of Athena. Most of all I liked the illustration of her in the book, her helmet and those green eyes. Her gaze. She wasn't afraid of anything, and I, who was almost always afraid, was fascinated and comforted by her essence and her features. The goddess of wisdom and war. She was the wind in the sails of warriors leaving for battle, but only when she wanted to be. She wasn't forced into it. It was her choice. I wanted to be her.

Christian opened the door to my room.

Should we play chess?

Yes, I replied without thinking.

He walked ahead of me into the dayroom. He scattered the chess pieces on the table: a mix from two different chess boards, some bigger than others.

This one's a knight, Christian said, and pointed to a bishop with a note stuck to it that bore a red X.

Okay, I said.

This is a rook, he continued, and held up a pawn with an O written on it.

Yes, I said.

This is the queen, he continued, and did in fact show me a queen, though she'd been decapitated.

In here this all seemed perfectly reasonable. My dad would often sacrifice his queen during a game, and this was along those lines.

Anything else out of the ordinary? I said, mostly to delay the inevitable start of the game.

White or black? Christian asked.

Black, I replied quickly. I was somewhat

better at defense than I was at opening.

Christian opened with a pawn. I responded with a knight. He played another pawn.

I mimicked him and played my pawn.

A few quick moves without thinking. I wanted to clear the board as quickly as possible so I could castle. It always felt good to get the rook out.

I took the bishop and proceeded diagonally.

That's the knight, Christian said and pointed at the note with the red X.

I switched to a pawn.

We played awhile. Exchanging some pieces to make space. I wasn't under any illusions. I wasn't good at chess. Neither was Christian, but he was better than I was.

Check, I said.

Christian retreated with the king which he'd sent out for a wander without foreseeing the danger.

I took the rook. Christian didn't seem to notice what I was up to.

He made another meaningless move. I went in for the kill. I locked in the king with my other rook.

Checkmate.

Congratulations, Christian said. That was quick.

I was unbelievably happy. I'd won.

This was the second time I'd ever won a game of chess.

Could it be? Was I good at chess after all? This was a brand-new thought, but I didn't have a chance to think it through before the victory became a defeat. Here I am playing chess in a locked ward just like my father used to do.

I wonder if this pleased my father. Could he see me from his heaven? What did he think when he saw me? Was he happy or sad that I was sitting here repeating his actions? I bet God let him skip the line to Paradise.

Undoubtedly he'd have forgiven Dad right away for the mess he'd made while he was still alive. My father had innocent eyes, especially when you didn't know him, which God surely did not. My father had a knack for taking action when no one was looking.

The alarm went off. Maybe my dad had pulled it, to interrupt my thoughts.

Christian was already running through

the corridor. The care workers who had been nowhere in sight were suddenly everywhere.

If you were so inclined, these instances when everyone's attention was focused in a single direction could be taken advantage of. It was a weakness built into the system. I couldn't think of anything to do now that everybody was otherwise occupied, so instead I obediently placed the chess pieces back in the box.

A woman was screaming and flailing. I couldn't see her, but I heard the despair in her scream. A flock of people dressed in white were holding her down. She didn't know where she was. She was strong and kept slipping free. The despairing are incredibly strong. Thuds and shrieks, quickly silenced. She was probably already asleep on the floor after the injection. A not-uncommon occurrence.

She'd soon get used to being here and once she'd gotten so used to it that she no longer knew anything else, she'd be shown the door.

Business as usual.

It was nothing to pay attention to. I was unafraid but anxious. Faint pictures moved freely inside me. The summer was boiling hot. The winter indifferent. The dam drained of its water. Crows' leftovers on the path, rotten food, hatred held still in order to remain invisible. The most dangerous path. I never chose it.

Always these white feet and blood. A sight I've seen my entire life.

The spine stretches. I dream only this dream. I am the focal point of certain smiling people's sincere interest. What have I done? Yielded to their will. And then what? Nothing. One day I'll stop answering their questions; it will be the day they stop smiling. A hand on the back of my neck, it hurts, but I keep that to myself.

Are you leaving, too?

Too? What have I done?

We still don't have anything to say about you.

Doesn't matter, I proffered and looked around.

But you're disappointing us.

It can't be that bad, I ventured as I slowly

backed up. You don't need me like I need myself. I'm terminating my contract.

I'm not here anymore. You can't see me. I'm deploying a smoke screen.

I wake up in my room. It doesn't hurt. I ask for nothing. I make it clear that all I'm asking for is to be allowed to leave my post.

I'm asking to be able to say thank you and goodbye.

Attilla laughs. How did he get here? Suddenly he's in my bed. Has anyone else seen him here in the ward? Are my thoughts this twitchy because he's here?

Attilla, I say.

What do you want, my child?

Why were you talking about me moving to a country across the sea?

I don't know, my child. It seemed important at the time.

So nothing is constant?

You're beginning to tire. Good.

Lie down on the bed. All stretched out. Yes, like that.

Imagine you're by a mountain. You are ascending a path, to a ledge. You are alone. All alone this evening on the mountain.

You're breathing against the mountain. You're asking for advice.

What does the mountain say?

Follow the path. It's going to end well. Up the mountain like a little goat.

I walk along the path. The sky is unblinking and my legs hold. I feel mighty.

Are you on top of the mountain?

What do you take me for? Someone who'll sprint uphill?

Calm down. You're on the right side of reality.

Is this another séance?

Just a little relaxation.

I see. Yes. Well then. I fall asleep and dream of Attilla helping himself to tea and sitting down in order to read a book aloud for me. He's speaking a language I don't understand. How long am I asleep in that room?

How did Attilla get there? Am I really the only one who's met him? I get no answers. Presumably because I'm sleeping.

You're not as bad off as it seems, he says suddenly from far away in the dream. Then closer: It's going well. The sky sees you sleeping. When you wake up it will be time for you to go back home.

I'm asking you to wake up. One. Two. Three. I wake up.

What did you say to me in the dream?

I look around for him. He's nowhere. I can't ask after him either. Then they'll really think I've lost it.

I have full-body chills. There was something he'd said in the dream. I shut my eyes but find nothing.

To break the mood, I sit on the bed and take out the guitar. I switch between three chords until I've calmed down. I start singing a folk song. I sing louder. I can still sing. I get hot inside. This reunion is making me grandiose. I forge plans. I can start singing in a choir again. Altos are always needed. But do you have to be able to read sheet music? Why haven't I learned anything essential?

Then the next question: Will I be able to write again? Do I still have what it takes?

I flip through my notes. They're barely legible.

I take a seat on the chair by the table and try to read what I've written.

I make out two sentences. The first goes: *You are here on overtime.*

And the second: *Mangia bene, ridi spesso, ama molto.* Eat well, laugh often, love much. There you have it. When did I last laugh? Years ago, and nowadays I neither eat nor love.

Do I still love you? I search myself. No, us living apart is good. We got on each other's nerves.

I suddenly remember the kitten I trampled to death. I was walking in clogs out to the summerhouse at night. What was I going to do there? I was sleepwalking. I opened the door and stepped on it. Its little spine broke. I trampled it to death. It snapped underneath me. In the space of a moment I became a murderer. The other kittens bounded around me, rubbed up against me. I ran away, to you, woke you up and said:

I've killed a kitten.

You tore yourself from sleep, went out and took stock, lay back down and fell asleep. That sleep of yours. The second your head hit the pillow you were out. Total renewal.

I think that all presidents, all high-ranking heads of state, can sleep. I think it's a prerequisite. I think humanity can be split into those who can sleep and those who cannot.

All night I waited for you to open your eyes again.

What did you do with it? I asked, when you finally woke up.

I threw it in the trash, you said and got up.

In the trash?

If you'd wanted an honorable burial you could have dug a ditch, laid a few flowers, and sung a song, you said.

Actions and inactions. No one rewards you for goodwill. You shape the life you call your own with every passing second. One moment after the next.

I was a murderer. I had trampled a kitten to death. I hadn't wanted to, but I'd done it.

There were twelve of us at Dad's funeral. It was winter. I read a poem by Fröding: "Who takes a lanternman for a man with a lantern?"

Only I knew the words my dad and I had exchanged a few days before he died alone in his new apartment on New Year's Eve.

Were my words what had killed him?

There's a knock on the door. I get up. Christian says, Five minutes. I didn't know what I was waiting for. Electricity, or something else? What was I supposed to do in five minutes?

I stood in the corridor and tried to get rid of an insight. I searched my pocket. There was something there that I'd written. What did it say? I couldn't find it.

The night before, I'd played chess and won. I had beat Christian. Why was he standing there grinning? Hadn't I won? Why did I have to beat Christian? I was about to ask him who'd won yesterday's match, when a door opened at the far end of the corridor. It was me. I was the one coming out of the room with Maria and closing the door behind me. I was walking through the corridor. As I passed by I looked at myself like you might look at a thing in passing, gaze unfixed. I watched myself leave the ward.

I open the door, walk into the hall.

It smells like a house smells when no one has been there for a long time. I open the kitchen window. Sit down at the table.

I sit there a long time, twilight falls.

I force myself to go into the living room. There's an echo. My steps resonate. I can't stop there.

I walk up the stairs. Open the doors to the small rooms where the children will live. There are beds inside. How did they get there? Beds, small night tables and rugs. Ceiling lamps. Has somebody furnished the house? How did that happen? Only I have the key. Am I the one who's done this?

I look out the window from Olivia's room. I can see all the way down to the harbor. A ship rumbles before departure. I sit on the bed and stroke the coverlet. I sit like that until night comes. I light the bedside lamp, walk into the next room. I make Anna's bed and open the window. The night air finds its way in. Clear, cold. I move on to Josef's room. A loft bed with a writing desk underneath and a colorful rug. A small window.

I stand there holding the handle to the room I'll share with Sara. I tell myself to open the door. I don't. I end up standing there handle in hand. The headlights from the street sweep across the wall. I tell myself it's fine. The tears burn in my eyes. I open the door and enter the dark room.

I undress and let the garments fall to the floor.

I lie on my bed and cry for the first time in years. I cry for everything. For the children who are coming over for *fika* tomorrow. They'll arrive with the items they want to keep here. I cry for you and me.

I say the children's names aloud in the room. I say Anna, Olivia, Josef, and Sara.

SASKIA VOGEL was born and raised in Los Angeles and now lives in its sister city, Berlin, where she works as a writer and Swedish-to-English literary translator. Her translations include work by leading female authors, such as Katrine Marcal, Karolina Ramqvist, Lina Wolff, and the modernist eroticist Rut Hillarp. Her debut novel *Permission* was published in four languages in 2019.

On the Design

As book design is an integral part of the reading experience, we would like to acknowledge the work of those who shaped the form in which the story is housed.

Tessa van der Waals (Netherlands) is responsible for the cover design, cover typography, and art direction of all World Editions books. She works in the internationally renowned tradition of Dutch Design. Her bright and powerful visual aesthetic maintains a harmony between image and typography and captures the unique atmosphere of each book. She works closely with internationally celebrated photographers, artists, and letter designers. Her work has frequently been awarded prizes for Best Dutch Book Design.

The image of the author on the cover was taken by Swedish photographer Jasmin Storch. She says of the encounter: "Linda came to my home one early afternoon last year. The sunlight was exceptionally strong that day and the air was cool. The sky was intensely blue. Not the ideal setup for a daylight shoot. I liked Linda straightaway, she had something elusive and phantasmic about her; she was easy to photograph, completely comfortable in front of the camera. I read her book six months later. The writing was raw and pure: unapologetic. I regret not having read it before we met."

The cover has been edited by lithographer Bert van der Horst of BFC Graphics (Netherlands).

Suzan Beijer (Netherlands) is responsible for the typography and careful interior book design of all World Editions titles.

The text on the inside covers and the press quotes are set in Circular, designed by Laurenz Brunner (Switzerland) and published by Swiss type foundry Lineto.

All World Editions books are set in the typeface Dolly, specifically designed for book typography. Dolly creates a warm page image perfect for an enjoyable reading experience. This typeface is designed by Underware, a European collective formed by Bas Jacobs (Netherlands), Akiem Helmling (Germany), and Sami Kortemäki (Finland). Underware are also the creators of the World Editions logo, which meets the design requirement that "a strong shape can always be drawn with a toe in the sand."